HEMINGWAY and the DEAD GODS

HEMINGWAY

and the
DEAD
GODS

A STUDY IN EXISTENTIALISM

John Killinger

University of Kentucky Press

Publication of this book is possible partly by reason of a grant from the Margaret Voorhies Haggin Trust established in memory of her husband James Ben Ali Haggin.

TO MY WIFE

FOREWORD

THIS IS A study of the fictional world of Ernest Hemingway as it is related to the world view of existentialism.

Properly speaking, Hemingway is not an existentialist, for there has been no known liaison between him and the existentialists, either personally or intellectually, and neither has ever formally recognized a kinship to the other.

It is entirely possible, of course, that the young American who lived in an attic where Verlaine had once lived, and who always loved Paris more than any other city in the world, imbibed the spirit of existentialism in the bars and bistros of that city in the nineteen-twenties. Sartre and most of the others who today form the vanguard of Parisian existentialism were then frequenting the same cabarets as Hemingway.

But it is more likely that the similarities in their world views are due not to collaboration but to living in the same milieu, and that Hemingway's philosophy of life, which appears already to have taken form in his earliest stories and sketches, and which therefore antedates every publication of both the German and the French existentialists, has not been affected by contact with this group of sophisticated thinkers, but has been the hard, wrung-from-the-heart product of life in an age which has been, in many ways, more difficult than any other. In a time when death is so mechanical and impersonal as to produce the *nada*-concept, when one of man's most profound fears is of nihilation by absorption into the machine, the mass, or whatever, it is not unlikely that many thinking men arrive independently at approximately the same conclusions about what it means to exist.

Charles Scribner's Sons have graciously permitted me to use quotations from the various works of Ernest Hemingway. In particular I wish to acknowledge their generosity in allowing me to quote extensively from *For Whom the Bell Tolls* (copyright 1940 by Ernest Hemingway) and from *Green Hills of Africa* (copyright 1953 by Ernest Hemingway).

J. K.

CONTENTS

FOREWORD   PAGE vii

CHAPTER 1. IN OUR TIME   1

CHAPTER 2. THE ROLE OF DEATH   17

CHAPTER 3. THE SIMPLE VERSUS THE
                COMPLICATED   33

CHAPTER 4. THE DEATH OF THE GODS   55

CHAPTER 5. THE ONE AND THE MANY   81

CHAPTER 6. THE HERO IN LOVE   89

            CONCLUSION   97

NOTES   103

INDEX   111

CHAPTER ONE

IN OUR TIME

THROUGHOUT all of his adult life, Ernest Hemingway has been convinced that our time is somehow more difficult than all previous times. One of his earliest works appeared under the title of *In Our Time*, a phrase that Philip Young suspects was sardonically borrowed from the Prayer Book's "Give peace in our time, O Lord."[1] The cover for the limited first edition of the book was a pastiche of chaotically placed newspaper clippings, with headlines like "Common Malady is Found Serious Among Women Here," "Comment Va-t-on Declarer La Prochaine Guerre?," and "General Public Barred from Film on Obstetrics," all emphasizing the break between our time and the past.[2] Our time is a time of violence and brutality to exceed that of all other times. "Fa brutto tempo," says the night porter at the Gritti to Colonel Cantwell in *Across the River and into the Trees*. "Bruttissimo," replies the Colonel. That macabre little sketch, "A Natural History of the Dead," is described as "the Whittier's *Snow Bound* of our time."[3] "I think we are born into a time of great difficulty," says Robert Jordan in *For Whom the Bell Tolls*. "I think any other time was probably easier . . . it is a time of difficult decisions."

This extreme sense of contemporaneity, which George Snell

lists as a major reason for Hemingway's literary popularity,[4] is also one of the hallmarks of a vigorous philosophical movement of our time, a movement broadly known as existentialism. For the existentialists, as for Hemingway's Nick Adams or Frederick Henry, the only peace for our time is the "separate peace," the nervous, tenuous half-peace which can be won only by the individual and must be won over and over again.

Perhaps "existentialism" is only a Tiffany word for a Woolworth concept, but it serves as a convenient tag for the thought of any writer who is more than ordinarily concerned about what it means to exist. A full understanding of the word involves a knowledge of its Latin roots *ex sistere*, from *ex stare*, a phrase meaning "to stand out." The primary concern of those who have been called existentialists is that the individual human being "stand out" as an individual, separated from all other being, human or non-human.

This concern is by no means new. Socrates has been called an existentialist because he seemed continually to reduce human life to its simplest terms. There is obvious similarity between Stoicism and existentialism, especially in the ethics of the two philosophies. Many Christian existentialists regard Jesus as an existentialist because he put such a premium on individualism and refused to be absorbed into the religious traditions of his fathers. Shakespeare's Hamlet was inordinately concerned about the meaning and tone of man's existence, and has received critical interpretation from an existentialist viewpoint.[5] Thoreau established himself at Walden in order to come to terms with the question of basic existence and to see what a man might learn from living in that purified state. In almost every age, in fact, there has probably been someone who might be called an existentialist.

The acknowledged father of existential philosophy in our day, though, is Søren Kierkegaard, who was born in Copenhagen in 1813. His was the age of Hegel, and of the cantilever method in philosophy. Hegel's golden system was the ultimate in human speculation; farther than this, men thought, human reason could never go. It stood like a great glistening palace beside the lath-and-stucco dwellings of all previous philosophers.

But Kierkegaard was not impressed by philosophers who set up such breathtaking structures and then content themselves with living in mere huts.[6] Speculating academicians, he said, can never explain life, because they separate themselves from it in order to think or to become books.[7] He once characterized thought that is abstract as "thought without a thinker."[8] It is an unforgivable sin to lose the individual in the labyrinth of the Hegelian dialectic. After all, if philosophy does not serve man, of what use is it?

Kierkegaard studied in Germany. But he went home to become the gadfly of Copenhagen and, like his Athenian predecessor, to work at the role of philosophical midwifery. He had no system of his own to propound, nor did he wish to become the darling of a cult. What he wanted was to clear the air of all the stagnant thought that had cloyed it since the time of the early Greeks, with the hope that the fresh air would awaken his fellow citizens to the full value of their own personalities and to the importance of filling those personalities with real and meaningful acts and thoughts. To this end he harried the established Church of Denmark and wrote more than a dozen of the century's most stimulating books in less than ten years.

Yet Kierkegaard did not become popular in his own day. His works were published in Germany, but even there he was not recognized as important until the nineteen-twenties. So, with the exception of Nietzsche, whose Superman polemics are well known, and Dostoievski, the Russian Dionysiac, pure existential thought leapt historically from 1855, the year of Kierkegaard's death, to the publication of Martin Heidegger's *Sein und Zeit, Erste Hälfte* in 1927.

Sein und Zeit remains Heidegger's greatest work (although he has never produced the second half) and the major academic document of existentialism in this century. It has not, however, been translated into either French or English because of the extreme difficulty of Heidegger's style; he writes a kind of Deutschen Carlylese strange even to many German readers.[9] As a result, he has not received internationally the attention really due him, and the most popular representative of existentialism has been a Frenchman, Jean-Paul Sartre.

Because of his rather colorful history as a member of the Resistance and as a Nazi prisoner during World War II, and because he has chosen to propagate his ideas through novels and dramas as much as through the more conventional philosophical forms, Sartre has been regarded by some as a gifted opportunist merely capitalizing on an amateurish grasp of philosophical problems. But actually his background is quite respectable, including even a period of study under Heidegger and a professorship at the Sorbonne, and his 700-page major opus, *L'Être et le néant*, is far from amateurish.

His ability to write philosophy like good fiction is doubtless the key to his popularity, which has expanded almost to the proportions of a fad even in America. He has been decried in the more "correct" journals for vulgarizing philosophy by putting a diluted form of it into the hands of the man on the street.[10] But if existentialism stands for anything it stands for putting philosophy within the reach of the average individual, and a conscientious examiner of Sartre's philosophy must admit that, whether it is right or wrong, it is anything but cheap; its demands are fully as strenuous as those of any extreme form of idealism.

More recently, Sartre's position of leadership among the existentialists has been seriously threatened, if not overtaken, by the youngish but profound figure of Albert Camus, who was such an uncompromising individualist that he even refused to be called an existentialist. Camus too was a prolific *littérateur*, balancing his time between serious essays and extremely respectable fiction (he received the Nobel Prize for Literature in 1957).

Camus' refusal to be classed with the existentialists stemmed from the rigidity with which he held to the principle of the individual's revolt. "The universe which Camus has described," says Thomas Hanna, "is limited by death and man's estrangement from the world, and Camus calls for a refusal of the world which is not a renouncement and which means having 'the conscious certainty of a death without hope.' "[11] In other words, Camus (or his ideal character) lives in revolt against his own finitude. Certain existentialists, however, Kierkegaard and Jaspers among them, while they emphasize man's finitude, take an irrational "leap of faith," and call the relationship between the finite and the infinite "God." This, as far as Camus is concerned, amounts to "philosophical suicide." He shuns both real suicide and philosophical suicide, and makes his hero live in constant revolt against his situation in the world. As he declared in his Nobel Prize acceptance speech, a writer's first duty is to refuse to lie about what he knows to be true—and, for him, to bridge humanism and theism is wholly unjustifiable, because, at least since Kant's *Critique of Pure Reason* appeared, such a feat is impossible of even the feeblest substantiation.

Despite this reluctance to be typed with the existentialists, though, Camus is almost universally regarded as a leading exponent of the existential viewpoint, for he continually exhibited, in both his essays and his fiction, characteristics in harmony with the general world view and spirit of the best of existentialism.

It is possible that Camus' differences merely illustrate a rather conspicuous absence of plan and program among the existentialists. Because existentialism is by its very nature a way of thinking and not a system, there is an inevitable confusion of tongues among its leading thinkers, with Paris generally regarded as its Babel. Names like Beauvoir, Berdyaev, Buber, Bultmann, Jaspers, Marcel, Maritain, Ortega, Tillich and Unamuno, as well as Heidegger and Sartre and Camus, all belong to an international roll call of existentialism, but a unified outline of their thought is practically impossible.

Even a general attempt to trace the similarities and influences in their works, not to mention those of their scores or even hundreds of devotees and imitators, would appear as an impenetrable network of crisscrossing lines and vectors. Consequently, most studies of existentialism have been historical in their approach rather than cross-referent.

Still, all is not hopeless in this modern pandemonium. Despite the multitude of dissimilarities in the works of these thinkers, they have but one method of approach, which varies so infrequently that such occasions merely prove the rule. That method of approach is the reduction of all knowledge to the very simplest facts. And for the convenience of the reader who has had no prior acquaintance with the existentialist literature, the simplest facts may arbitrarily be reduced to three, which are common to practically all of the existentialists —an individual, a fundamental choice, and a way of life.

I.

The basic attempt of all existentialism has been to establish the separate identity of the individual. To accomplish this end, it has warred, at various times, on practically every collective movement aimed at destroying the uniqueness of the individual and at incorporating him into a larger entity. For Kierkegaard, the enemy was corporate Christianity; for Nietzsche, it was the inverted morality of submission; for Jaspers, it has been the conformity brought about by life in a technological age; for Beauvoir, it has been a collective ethics. And existentialism proclaims the evangel of freedom in an effort to deliver man from the anonymity of the mass, whether the mass be a philosophical system, a state, a culture, or a religion. As Francis Jeanson said in opening a discussion among several Parisian existentialists, "Existentialism constitutes an effort to rehabilitate man in his own eyes, to restore him to himself."[12]

Miguel de Unamuno has described the kind of man in whom the existentialists are interested. He is

The man of flesh and bone; the man who is born, suffers, and
dies—above all, who dies; the man who eats and drinks and plays
and sleeps and thinks and wills; the man who is seen and heard;
the brother, the real brother.

They have no real feelings about the other kind,

the legendary featherless biped, the ζῶον πολιτικόν of Aristotle, the
social contractor of Rousseau, the *homo economicus* of the Man-
chester School, the *homo sapiens* of Linnaeus, or, if you like, the
vertical mammal. A man neither of here nor there, neither of this
age nor of another, who has neither sex nor country, who is, in brief,
merely an idea. That is to say, a no-man.[13]

Traditional philosophy was powerless to free the individual;
instead, it swallowed him up, brainwashed him, and left him
thinking he was only "a puny part of the great whole." That
was why Kierkegaard first repudiated Hegel's impressive
system of philosophical panpsychism. More recently, Simone
de Beauvoir too rejected Hegel as irrelevant. She wrote of
having experienced a "great feeling of calm" on reading Hegel
in the cold, impersonal setting of the Bibliothèque Nationale
in August, 1940. "But," she complained, "once I got into the
street again, into my life, out of the system, beneath a real
sky, the system was no longer of any use to me: what it had
offered me, under a show of the infinite, was the consolations
of death; and I again wanted to live in the midst of living
men."[14]

This distrust of impersonal systems may be in part responsible for the philosophical method of the existentialists, a
method so loosely organized that many professional philosophers have arbitrarily dismissed it as hackwork, or as the
dime-novel genre of philosophy. But for thinkers who are
passionately concerned with the individual, the presentation
of their thought seems logically to assume the more personal
forms of journalism. Kierkegaard's major works read like the
thoughts of an Hebraic Pascal; practically all of Nietzsche's

writings are aphoristic; Unamuno's *Tragic Sense of Life* looks
like a notebook put into print without warning to the author;
and Gabriel Marcel writes his books as diaries and frankly
labels them journals. This passion to connect philosophical
thought with real life has doubtless led, too, to the vogue of
philosophical novels and plays. It is impossible to imagine
Hegel ever being translated into a novel; yet the major
propagation of Jean-Paul Sartre's philosophy has not been
through the massive *L'Être et le néant* but through half a
dozen best-selling novels and widely read plays.

In the Middle Ages, it was almost exclusively the Church
that devoured individualism in the Western world. But in
our time there are other forms of mass life more to be feared.
In fact, the whole culture of modern times appears to be
threatening to swallow up the individual. Karl Jaspers has
insistently warned the world against the *masse-Mensche,* the
man who so completely accepts the culture of his age that he
loses his individuality. "We are on the road," he says "to a
functional absorption of all men in the machine."[15] At times
Jaspers appears merely to be lending the dignity of philosophy
to the "brave new world" motif, but it may well be that his
fears are justified. At least, many provocative writers, including
non-existentialists William H. Whyte and Erich Fromm, have
in recent years attempted to document the passing of man's
individuality. Whyte's popular sociological study, *The Organization Man,* spells out the frightening effects of Leavittown
living on the average American mind. He demonstrates in the
areas of education, business, domestic relations, community
management, recreation, religion, etc., the readiness of most
Americans to accept without question the standards of the
group.

Fromm has been especially interested in the problem of
man's psychological isolation from his fellows, and in his
attempts to overcome his sense of separateness. In primitive
religions, sexual orgies were designed for overcoming separateness; when one began to feel alone again, the orgy was simply

repeated. In our society, says Fromm, the orgy has been replaced by alcoholism, drug addiction, private sexual orgasm, and conformity, which is probably the most frequently used method. "In contemporary Western society," Fromm says,

the union with the group is the prevalent way of overcoming separateness. It is a union in which the individual self disappears to a large extent, and where the aim is to belong to the herd. If I am like everybody else, if I have no feelings or thoughts which make me different, if I conform in custom, dress, ideas, to the pattern of the group, I am saved; saved from the frightening experience of aloneness.[16]

Salvation at this price is, to the existentialist, no salvation at all. On the contrary, it is the very damnation to hell which Sartre has described in his play *No Exit*.

Gabriel Marcel accuses even modern analytical psychology of joining the conspiracy to obliterate the individual. It teaches too strictly that man is an amalgamation of functions operating on a time-table, and omits the possibility of any of Marcel's beloved "mysteries" in life. Traveling on the subway, he says,

I often wonder with a kind of dread what can be the inward reality of the life of this or that man employed on the railway—the man who opens the doors, for instance, or the one who punches the tickets. Surely everything both within him and outside him conspires to identify this man with his functions—meaning not only his functions as worker, as trade union member or as voter, but with his vital functions as well. The rather horrible expression "time table" perfectly describes his life. So many hours for each function. Sleep too is a function which must be discharged so that the other functions may be exercised in their turn. The same with pleasure and relaxation; it is logical that the weekly allowance of recreation should be determined by an expert on hygiene; recreation is a psycho-organic function which must not be neglected any more than, for instance, the function of sex. We need go no further; this sketch is sufficient to suggest the emergence of a kind of vital schedule; the details will vary with the country, the climate, the profession, etc., but what matters is that there is a schedule.[17]

And the existentialists abhor schedules. None of the characters in Sartre's plays and novels lives in a pattern; one may search all his works in vain for an ordinary person who goes to a job regularly for eight hours a day and then comes home punctually for an evening meal and the papers. In fact, they seem lost in this world. But it may be that we are all lost, and that they alone are conspicuously lost because they are searching for themselves, because they dare to be individuals.

II.

Every man faces the choice of being a genuine individual or of being just part of the crowd. This choice is fundamental to the thinking of every existentialist. For Kierkegaard, it was a choice between living *comically* and living *vitally*. The comical man plays all his life at being something he is not. He may be a priest who has lost faith and fears the opinions of others if he renounces the frock, or he may be a banker who has always wished to be a store clerk, but in either case he is a comical man because he goes on hypocritically in the wrong role. The vital man, on the other hand, is the man who discovers the distinctive essence of his own being and pursues it as his life, defending it as inalienable from his very existence.

Martin Heidegger's corresponding division is between natural objects (*Vorhandenheit*) and human life (*Dasein*). Technically, all men belong to the category of *Dasein;* but those who do not choose to live as individuals are behaving in the manner of the *Vorhandenheit.* For example, a writer who chooses to starve, if necessary, in order to continue to write pure art possesses true *Dasein;* but an equally gifted writer who is willing to sell out his integrity for a regular income from a pulp magazine has placed himself in a position of abjectness not very different from the *Vorhandenheit* of any dependent material object. True "being-there" is a matter of real individuality, of choosing to be one's highest and best self despite the consequences. Heidegger calls the man who deliberately posits himself as *Dasein* and maintains himself as such by constant effort the "authentic" man. It is the highest word of praise he can bestow on any man.

For Sartre, the distinction lies between being-in-itself (*l'être-en-soi*) and being-for-itself (*l'être-pour-soi*). Being-in-itself is the quality of objective nature; being-for-itself is proper to the subjective being. Man should of course belong to the category of the for-itself. But if he seeks to escape the responsibility of human freedom, willfully retreating into the in-itself, he thereby assumes the nature of material objects subject to regular cause-and-effect laws. The man who exists as *pour-soi* Sartre speaks of as "sincere"; the man who attempts to get by as *en-soi,* on the other hand, behaves in "bad faith" (*la mauvaise foi*) with the world.

Sartre illuminates the concept of the existential choice with the rather pedestrian illustration of a man poised on the brink of a cliff, looking down into a dizzying abyss. Suddenly he realizes with penetrating insight that he is free to fall upon the rocks below and perish, or, by carefully choosing his way, to go on living. These are his possibilities. At the moment, they are equally balanced, and he takes to himself the Godlike attribute of self-determination: that possibility will prevail to which he lends his support. The realization comes as a cathartic experience, opening up the whole of life to the same vital question of existence. He is free to be or not to be.[18]

III.

In this world, where a man can thus choose to be himself or to remain anonymous, good and evil become mere qualities of the way of life which the individual chooses. Here existentialism approaches classicism, because each conceives of value and disvalue "not as properties or essences, but rather as modes of existence. Evil is to act and to exist in a warped and privative way; good is to act in accordance with nature—to exist authentically in the highest degree."[19]

To be sure, the choice of one's self is by far the harder choice. It is much more difficult to be a waiter who behaves as an individual than to be Sartre's waiter who walks like a waiter, serves like a waiter, and generally affects the obsequious appearance of a waiter as the world conceives of the idea of a waiter.[20] The crowd, be it a social group, a political organization, or a Sunday School class, is invariably suspicious of the individual. Camus calls him *l'homme révolté*, the rebel, and rebels are never welcome. They are too much of a threat to the established order and to the comfort of persons less vital than themselves. This is why one writer has identified the essential mood of existentialism as "the homelessness of man,"[21] and it explains Heidegger's fondness for the "wanderer" poems of Hölderin.[22] The true existentialist is a pilgrim without a place to rest. He is the *isolato*, like Gregor Samsa in Kafka's "Metamorphosis." He is the outsider to society, like Meursault in Camus' *The Stranger*.

The otherness of Samsa is struck in the very first paragraph of "Metamorphosis," when he awakens and finds that he has been transformed into a huge bug, incapable of communicating with his family or his employers. For the horrible remainder of his life, he and the rest of the world are *incommunicado*, and at times even hostile. The basic differences between him and those around him have always inwardly existed, but the metamorphosis has permanently crystallized and objectified them.

Camus' Meursault, in a flash of psychosomatic blindness, shoots and kills an Arab in what is not clearly an open-and-shut case of self-defense. But the prosecution, rather than present the real facts of the murder, rests its case upon a number of wholly unrelated incidents which serve to mark Meursault as an individual. The director of the home for the aged where his mother died testifies that he did not weep at his mother's

funeral, and that he smoked and drank coffee during her wake.
Other witnesses establish that, on the day following the funeral,
he went swimming with a new girl friend, took her to see the
latest Fernandel comedy, and then spent the night with her
at his apartment. Moreover, he admits his friendship with a
man who is generally suspected, though it has never been
proved, of the act of procuring.

Through most of the trial, Meursault sits as though he were
living in another world. Once he pricks up his ears and hears
his defense lawyer saying, "It is true I killed a man." The
lawyer continues in the same vein, saying "I" each time he
refers to the accused. This strikes Meursault as peculiar, and
he leans over to ask a gendarme about it. The gendarme
answers that they all do the same thing. But to Meursault, it
seems that "the idea behind it was still further to exclude me
from the case, to put me off the map, so to speak, by sub-
stituting the lawyer for myself. Anyway, it hardly mattered;
I already felt worlds away from this courtroom and its tedious
'proceedings.' "[23]

When the jury finds him guilty "in the name of the French
people,"—Meursault thinks it almost humorous that people
who do such personal things as change their underwear should
credit a decision over human life to such a vague entity as
"the French people," and that they might as well have said
"the German people" or any other people—it is the pronounce-
ment of general society upon every authentic individual who
ever has or ever will pass as a stranger through its midst.[24]

This hard philosophy, offering nothing but anguish and a
tantalizing hunger for an authenticity that must be rewon
moment by moment, challenging even in its severity, is
especially forged to the temper of the modern man. The rapid
advance of technological science, the exhausting devastation
of two global wars, the intellectual discrediting of traditional
orthodoxy in religion, and the Nietzschean transmutation of

ethical values have spiritually and ethically marooned modern man even in the company of his brothers. Cast up Crusoe-like on the reef of a new world, he must gather up what is useful and what he is able to carry from the past and begin the lonely task of reconstruction. It is truly the day of the "separate peace."

Sartre frankly admits that the tension under which the existentialist lives is anguish (*l'angoisse*). It is agonizing because the all-important choice of being or not being one's self is posed not once for all but continuously. Heidegger's term for the concept (which he really borrowed from Kierkegaard and elaborated) is *das Angst*. It is the mood which brings men face to face with nothingness. It is neither anxiety (*Aengstlichkeit*) nor fear (*Furcht*); we are "afraid" of definite things, but dread is of something in particular. It is really not *of* something, but *about* something, and the something is indefinite. One merely feels something uncanny.[25]

"Nothingness" is a convenient designation for the inexplicable weirdness that lies beyond the rational boundaries of existence. Sartre, instead of speaking of it as "out there," as if it were something spatial rather than qualitative, says it lies coiled like a worm at the very heart of all true existence.[26] There is really no adequate definition of nothingness, nor any complete understanding of it; although Sartre devotes the entire first chapter of *L'Être et le néant* (over fifty pages) to an explanation of the term, the best he can say is that it is the contrary of what is phenomenological, or that it is simply what is not. As such, though, it continually threatens to annihilate man, to engulf and to snuff out his true existence.

The Spanish term for nothingness, which frequently appears in Unamuno's *Tragic Sense of Life*, is *nada*. Readers of Hemingway will remember how this significant little word dominates the celebrated short story, "A Clean, Well-Lighted Place." Hemingway even parodies the Ave Maria as "Hail nada, full of nada," and the Paternoster as "Our nada, which art in nada, nada be thy name." He seems to feel that in our

time that area of life which was once served by religion is
better served by the concept of *nada*.

The use of the term is not extraneous to the theme of the
story, but is linked inseparably to the haunting oblivion which
envelops all that is outside the pale of the little clean, well-
lighted place. And an arc of the *nada*-circle, says Professor
Baker, "runs all the way through Hemingway's work from the
night-fears of Jake Barnes to the 'horrorous' of Philip Rawlings
and the ingrowing remorse of Richard Cantwell."[27]

Baker himself has a feeling for the word *nada*, and writes
penetratingly of Hemingway's use of it:

> For the old waiter, the word *nothing* (or *nada*) contains huge
> actuality. The great skill displayed in the story is the development,
> through the most carefully controlled understatement, of the young
> waiter's mere *nothing* into the old waiter's Something—a Something
> called Nothing which is so huge, terrible, overbearing, inevitable,
> and omnipresent that, once experienced, it can never be forgotten.
> Sometimes in the day, or for a time at night in a clean, well-lighted
> place, it can be held temporarily at bay. What links the old waiter
> and the old patron most profoundly is their brotherhood in arms
> against this beast in the jungle.[28]

I believe that this *nada* as used by Hemingway is basically
the Nothingness of the existentialists, the strange, unknowable,
impending threat of nihilation, the *Nichts* of Heidegger, the
néant of Sartre, and the *nada* of Unamuno. And Hemingway
need not be a philosopher to employ the idea, because it is not
properly the matter of traditional philosophy at all.

The only entity truly capable of defying the encroachments
of Nothingness is the individual, and it goes without saying
that Hemingway, again like the existentialists, has always
exalted the lone man. No writer's protagonists are more
consistently referred to as heroes; most critics, in fact, have
found the phrase "Hemingway's heroes" to be an almost
inevitable cliché in practically everything they have written
about his work. The superior male ranks fully as important

in his world as the knight of faith, the authentic individual, the sincere being and the man in revolt in the worlds of Søren Kierkegaard, Martin Heidegger, Jean-Paul Sartre and Albert Camus, respectively.

There are also in Hemingway's thought other elements vital to existentialist thought, such as the bifurcation of life into the authentic and the unauthentic; the moment of existential choice, in which a man decides to be either authentic or unauthentic; and, in nontheistic existentialism, the exaltation of a humanistic ethic and the transmutation of aesthetics to the level where it becomes confused with ethics and a low kind of spirituality. That there are demonstrable affinities between Hemingway and the existentialists at these points—and others perhaps less important—is the substance of the following chapters.

I have no intention of tailoring Hemingway into a poor man's Heidegger, or of bestowing philosophical significance on the fiction of a man who would be the first to deny that he is a philosopher. But, without pressing his works into unnatural configurations, I hope to establish an interpretation of his world view that is both plausible and consistent—plausible enough to win even from the critic with an adamant preconceived interpretation an admission of the tenability of this one, and consistent enough for the more abstract conclusions drawn here to prove a helpful introduction to the interpretation of any further work from the pen of Mr. Hemingway.

CHAPTER TWO

THE ROLE OF DEATH

THE MOST obviously recurrent motif in all of Hemingway's work has been the subject of death, or of violence, which, as Frederick Hoffman has observed,[1] is only another form of death in which the victim survives. It began in the early story "Indian Camp," where little Nick watches his father perform a jack-knife Caesarean on an Indian squaw and then sees her buck, who could not bear the presence of suffering, lying in the bunk above her, with his throat cut and the blood gurgling from the wound. It still appeared strong in *The Old Man and the Sea*, nearly thirty years later, where the sun-baked old Santiago spends a restless night battling the *galanos* that relentlessly tear away the flesh of his fish.

Thomas Cash Jr., writing on Hemingway and death, began with a quotation from Granville Hicks: "All of Hemingway's compulsions stem from his feeling about death, with which he has been concerned in a way that few authors have since John Donne posed for a sculptor, wrapped in his winding sheet."[2] "Indeed," continues Cash himself,

it would be difficult to find an author who has written of death as often and as consistently as has Hemingway. At one time or another he has described the death of ants, salamanders, grass-

hoppers, and fish; how hyenas die, how to kill *kudu,* the proper way
to execute horses, how bulls are slain, how soldiers die, death in
Italy, in Cuba, in Africa and in Spain, death in childbirth and
death by suicide, death alone and death in a group; selfish death,
sacrificing death, and graceful death.

Because of this intense preoccupation with death in all its
forms, the discovery of the role which death plays in Hemingway's fiction is the most immediate key to the interpretation
of his work.

One of the most significant stories in which violence plays
a major part is the little sketch which formed Chapter VI of
In Our Time. There Nick Adams has become a young man
and has gone off to war. During a shelling he is seriously
wounded in the spine, where the neural movements are
coordinated. It affects him, as Philip Young has observed, both
physically and mentally.[3] "Senta Renaldi," he says. "Senta.
You and me we've made a separate peace. . . . Not patriots."

The wound has traumatically separated him from all other
being. Suddenly he is *not* a patriot. He will no longer seek
objectivity in the abstract and meaningless noun "patriotism,"
nor in an army of ciphers where the responsibility does not
rest with the individual. Violence has isolated him from the
formless lump of humanity—he *ex-sists.*

Here then is the core of Hemingway's philosophy of violence:
in the blinding flash of a shell, in the icy-burning impact of a
bullet, in the dangerous vicinity of a wounded lion, in the
sudden contact of a bull's horn, in that ill-defined twilight
between life and imminent death where time and place are
irrelevant questions, man faces his freedom. Nothing has any
meaning at that instant except survival and existence. The
superfluities of culture, race, tradition, even religion, all disappear in the face of one overpowering fact—the necessity to
exist on an individual basis. This is the "separate peace," the
only peace which can be won in our time.

This vision of death plays the same important part in the

philosophies of all the leading existentialists. For Kierkegaard, as for traditional Christian theology from St. Paul on, death and sin are in a sense synonymous, and it is sin that defines us from God: "No man can know God without becoming a sinner."[4] In other words, it is the death in sin that isolates us from the God of life, that creates us individuals and not mystically incorporated parts of the Godhead, and we never learn true worship until we learn to be alone before God. Death, says Kierkegaard in turn, is "the test of earnestness."[5] Earnestness is sincerity, or, in the Latin, *sine ceras*, "the absence of wax"—it is the purity of existence. Death tests this purity, as it did in the revelation of Nick Adams.

One of Karl Jaspers' most important theories is that of the "limit-situation."[6] Limit-situations are those in which we must either develop into something larger and finer or lose our souls, situations where we face a crisis-decision as Nick Adams faced his. And the foremost limit-situations are death, suffering, conflict, and guilt.[7] Death forces us to forgo the demand for an explanation of.everything and to concentrate on giving meaning to life through action.

Sartre has never expressly stated that it is death that reveals freedom to man; rather, man meets nothingness and freedom in the moment of anguish. Yet Sartre is inclined to illustrate anguish with portraits of men who find freedom as they face the possibility of death. In *Being and Nothingness*, for example, freedom appears to the man poised over an abyss. And it appears in a similar fashion to Mathieu Delarue in *The Reprieve*. He stands on the Pont Neuf, looking down into the murky waters of the Seine, contemplating dropping:

All hawsers cut, nothing now could hold him back: here was his freedom, and how horrible it was! Deep down within him he felt his heart throbbing wildly; one gesture, the mere unclasping of his hands, and *I would have been Mathieu*. Dizziness rose softly over the river; sky and bridge dissolved: nothing remained but himself and the water; it heaved up to him and rippled round his dangling legs. The water, where his future lay. At the moment *it is true*, I'm going to kill myself. Suddenly he *decided* not to do it. He decided: it shall merely be a trial. Then he was again upon his feet and walking on, gliding over the crest of a dead star. Next time, perhaps.[8]

In the face of death, freedom; life is reduced to its simplest terms, and the way is cleared for the future.

The same theme is played upon, with variations, in *Les Mouches,* where Orestes finds himself through slaying his mother and the king, and in *Huis Clos,* where the hell in which Garcin, Estelle and Inez find themselves is the final solidification of their three miserable lives, each now viewed by the other two and leading to the conclusion that "hell is other people," with not another chance to become real individuals because there is no more death. And it appears in the masterful scene at the end of *Iron in the Soul* (the third volume in the series begun by *The Age of Reason* and *The Reprieve*), where Mathieu at last finds the greatest kind of freedom when he deliberately engages himself in a death-situation for his fellow guerrillas by holding a tower singlehandedly against the enemy, the metal flying wildly around him and he gloriously shouting invectives all the while.

In Heidegger's *Sein und Zeit,* one of the most important concepts uniting the basic categories of "being" and "time" is *das Sein zum Tode,* or "the being toward death." It is a possibility belonging to human being (*Dasein*), never to other kinds of being (*vorhanden* or *zuhanden*), in which one mentally runs forward to death, or fully anticipates death. And it is in this running forward to death that one diminishes the false importance which has been assumed by the trivia of everyday existence (*die Alltäglichkeit*). To refuse to be *das Sein zum Tode* is to retreat into the unauthentic, the meaningless day-to-day existence, the *Verfallen.* That is, *das Sein zum Tode* serves the same purpose as Nick's spine wound: it reduces care (*Sorge*) and reveals the way to authenticity (*Eigentlich-*

keit). It is what happens in the story of Tolstoy's Iván Ilyich when Iván learns he is going to die: he must face the question, "Has my life been worthwhile?," and, if the answer is negative, he must transform himself into that which is worthwhile.

A similar reduction of life to the simplest facts is likewise vital to the thought of Albert Camus, and it led him to distill all philosophy to the problem of suicide:

> There is but one truly serious philosophical problem and that is suicide. Judging whether life is or is not worth living amounts to answering the fundamental question of philosophy. All the rest— whether or not the world has three dimensions, whether the mind has nine or twelve categories—comes afterwards. These are games; one must first answer.[9]

read J.D. Salinger's "A perfect day for banana fish" or Teddy

Yes, one must first answer, like Rambert the journalist in Camus' *La Peste*, the novel about the plague-stricken port of Oran in Algeria. When the city is quarantined, Rambert is shut up with the vermin-borne death like all the others, even though he is a stranger in the city and has a wife in France he stands to lose if he doesn't return. Eagerly he begins transactions with a go-between for two guards who will let him out through the gate one night. Then he meets the guards themselves, and moves into their residence to be near the gate. But when it is all finally arranged, and the very night is set for the escape—he decides to stay. Facing death on every hand for weeks has revealed his true self to him, and the possibility of escaping to the woman outside, previously such an obsession with him, has become a thing of little meaning beside the vital issue faced by the plague-ridden town of Oran. He decides to stay and join the fight against *la peste*.

There are many parallel situations in these and other existential works. These illustrations will suffice to establish the point that death has a central role in the philosophy of existentialism, and that that role is, as in Hemingway, to reduce the problem of existence to its lowest common denominator, where it can best be handled by man. Jaspers and his limit-situation, Mathieu on the Pont Neuf, Heidegger and *das Sein zum Tode*, Camus and his suicide question, and Nick Adams and his spine wound all arrive through the problem of death at the same destination—what it means to *ex-sist*.

Nick's spine wound, of course, is not an isolated instance of a Hemingway character facing death or violence. For Nick himself, it was merely the climax of a long acquaintance with the brutality of life, an acquaintance that began with the jack-knife Caesarean in the Indian camp. It was continued in "The Doctor and the Doctor's Wife," where Nick chooses to side with his father against the Indians rather than to believe, like his religious mother, that they are good men.

In "The Battler," Nick, in his teens, is cuffed off a moving freight train and falls into the cinders along the track. He stumbles dazedly into the camp of the old battler, a cauliflower-eared ex-fighter who becomes so pugnacious that the big Negro "Bugs" has to quiet him with a blow on the head.

In "The Killers," Nick has come to the big city, where he becomes involved with two professional assassins stalking a Swede, who sits and waits stoically for his death, convinced that any effort to escape would be futile.

Then he goes to war and sees violence in wholesale proportions: the officer who will not die but is put in the cave of the dead, in "A Natural History of the Dead"; the dead mules, lying in the water with their legs thrust at the sky, in "On the Quai at Smyrna"; and the two dead Austrians lying under a crumpled pink wall that had once hidden the now-twisted iron bedstead, in the story in which Nick receives the wound.

After the war, he goes to Spain. Every day he walks to the rehabilitation hospital to have his leg trained to bend again. There is one tall, pale-faced lieutenant there of whom Nick later says: "He had lived a very long time with death and was a little detached. We were all a little detached, and there was nothing that held us together except that we met every afternoon at the hospital."[10] Death had repeated its isolating function on each of them.

While in Spain, Nick sees the bullfights, which furnish material for several of the numbered sketches in *In Our Time* —material replete with violence. In Chapter IX there is the story of the torero who kills five bulls, then retches until his face is completely blanched. In Chapter X appears the wounded horse, cantering around the arena while his entrails oscillate comically from the wound beneath him. And in Chapter XII the great bull himself roars blood.

Back in the States again in the story "Fathers and Sons," Nick reflects on his father's suicide, which troubled him a great deal as a boy and which he comes to understand, though not pardon, as Robert Jordan in *For Whom the Bell Tolls.*

Nick does not appear by name in any of Hemingway's novels. But he passes through them all, wounded somehow in each. In *The Sun Also Rises* he is Jake Barnes, emasculated by the war. In *A Farewell to Arms* he is Frederick Henry, wounded by an exploding mortar in a fashion that reads almost verbatim like the account of Hemingway's own wounding as an ambulance driver. In *For Whom the Bell Tolls* he is Jordan, reflecting on the Negro he had seen lynched when he was a child, and still thinking about being handed the gun with which his father had committed self-murder.

In *Across the River and into the Trees* he is Richard Cantwell, who bears his share of wounds, still regrets losing a regiment because of stupid orders from higher up, and has seen plenty of war and death—sights like a G.I. lying in the road and being run over by every vehicle in the line moving up until his body was removed for the sake of morale, or like a dog and cat gnawing on the bodies of Germans who had been cooked alive by the white phosphorous dropped in advance of the Allies.

And in *The Old Man and the Sea* there is still the protagonist who holds tight against pain. "I must hold his pain where it is," thinks Santiago as he grips the line on his fish. "Mine does not matter. I can control mine. But his pain could drive him mad."

Philip Young has percipiently recognized the continuity of the wound:

The effect of the wounds Nick Adams has been suffering . . . is just beginning to be hinted at: this shell that has hit Nick in the spine is of a piece with the blows he took when he saw the jack-knife Caesarean, the nearly decapitated Indian, the battler, and the black-jacking Negro, when he felt himself forced to repudiate his mother and his girl friend, when he hit the cinders after a blow in the face on a freight train. This wound, which is to be the same wound which emasculates Jake in *The Sun Also Rises* and is to hospitalize Lt. Henry in *A Farewell to Arms,* and whose scar Col. Cantwell bears more than thirty years later in *Across the River and into the Trees,* is significant even beyond these facts.

From here on in, the Hemingway hero is to be a wounded man, wounded not only physically but—as soon becomes clear—psychically as well.[11]

And it is invariably the wound that sets him apart from all other men, that constitutes him an individual.

As Nick Adams, he is "a little detached." As Krebs, he looks at life from the front porch. As Jake Barnes, he is barred even from sexual relations. As Frederick Henry, he swims away from a war. As Harry Morgan, he will even murder his own shipmates to protect himself from the police. As Robert Jordan, he must cover the retreat of others. As Col. Cantwell, he hunts alone, and dies alone in the back of a car with a chauffeur who can never understand him because he, the chauffeur, has not experienced the wound. And as old Santiago, he fishes alone, by this somehow elevated above his beloved Dimaggio of the bone-spur, who, great as he is, plays the game with teammates.

I suspect Mr. Hemingway, in writing *The Old Man,* of having had in mind the composition of a *Moby-Dick* for "our

time," with one man against the fish rather than a boatload of
men of all faiths and bloods. In one of those in.pressive
symbolic scenes that come hard upon one another in Melville's epic, Ahab tempers a harpoon with the blood of
Tashtego, Queequeg and Daggoo, mingling the bloods of the
races; and from that moment on he draws them as one with
him after the white whale. His was the age of Hegel and the
system. But the old man of the sea, against an endless
expanse of sky and water, performs alone—not even the boy
is permitted to go with him. He is of our day, the day of the
separate peace.

There is just one catch to the fact that life receives its real
meaning when set over against death: for life to continue to
have meaning, the death experience must be repeated again
and again. The tension must be maintained, or the protagonist
ceases to be an individual and becomes part of the mass.

This is illustrated in Hemingway's short story "A Day's
Wait," in which nine-year-old Schatz thinks he is going to die
of influenza because he has a temperature of 102 degrees, and
he has heard that 44 degrees means certain death. The
gimmick, of course, is that the 102-degree reading is Fahrenheit
and the 44-degree reading is Centigrade. Until he learns of
his mistake, he faces the end with perfect control, and politely
asks his father to leave the room if it will bother him. But
afterwards, his hold over himself relaxes, and he cries very
easily at "little things that were of no importance."

The significant thing is that facing death (or so he thought)
made the little things unimportant to him, and that when
death was removed as an imminent threat, he relapsed into
ordinary childishness. To perpetuate the existentialist attitude,
it is necessary to continue to experience death and violence.

"An existing individual," said Kierkegaard, "is constantly in
the process of becoming; the actual existing subjective thinker
constantly reproduces this existential situation in his thoughts,
and translates all his thinking into terms of process."[12] One
of the characteristics of the Danish thinker's hero, his knight

of faith, is the continual experience of *Angst*: "Abraham is not Abraham without this dread."[13]

Camus, who thinks of the individual as a rebel, speaks of this perpetual tension as a "permanent revolution." Living

is keeping the absurd alive. Keeping it alive is above all contemplating it. Unlike Eurydice, the absurd dies only when we turn away from it. One of the only coherent philosophical positions is thus revolt. It is a constant confrontation between man and his own obscurity. It is an insistence upon an impossible transparency. It challenges the world anew every second.[14]

Sartre, too, is concerned that the crisis be felt every instant: "Man cannot be sometimes slave and sometimes free; he is wholly and forever free or he is not free at all."[15] He chooses himself at every moment, reconstituting the justification for his existence. This is illustrated clearly in Sartre's play *Morts sans sépulture,* where a group of Resistance prisoners is held for torture until their leader is revealed. Each of them is conscious of the need constantly to recreate his life, lest he spoil the lifetime that has gone before with one ignominious deed now. "It's not fair," complains Sorbier, "that a single minute should be enough to ruin a whole life." But it is, if it is the last.

The same accentuation of the present moment is seen in the case of the old man Santiago going to sea to prove his prowess to the boy again: "The thousand times he had proved it meant nothing. Now he was proving it again. Each time was a new time and he never thought about the past when he was doing it." Or in the words of Robert Jordan when he reflects that it is possible, provided you have reached a certain age, to live as full a life in seventy hours as in seventy years:

And if there is not any such thing as a long time, nor the rest of your lives, nor from now on, but there is only now, why then now is the thing to praise and I am very happy with it. Now, *ahora, maintenant, heute. Now,* it has a funny sound to be a whole world and your life.

Life is only an infinite succession of nows.

This abiding need to reconstitute the self, to evoke continually the individual by a repetition of the crisis-experience, is responsible in Hemingway for what many have deemed sheer belligerence. It is only by seeking war, by following the sores of battle as they break out around the world, now here, now there, that he can constantly reproduce this violence-catharsis.

Sigmund Freud spoke of this "repetition-compulsion" in connection with his famous theory of the death instinct. Freud first noted in children the tendency to repeat unpleasant episodes, in their case by play-acting. His work with traumatic-neurosis shock patients following World War I coincided with the discovery, and led to the formation of his celebrated theory that, counter to the life instinct in a person, there is also an opposing death instinct, or an abiding attempt of the organism to return to the nirvana of the prenatal state.[16]

It is unfortunate that Freud never wrote an essay on Hemingway's repetition-compulsion in relation to the death instinct, for Hemingway has been more ritualistic about death-seeking than almost any other figure in the modern world. Moreover, there are several prominent womb symbols in Hemingway's works (e.g., the water below the tracks in "The Battler," the river and the freight car in A Farewell to Arms, and the sleeping bag in For Whom the Bell Tolls) which accord with the death instinct and the desire for reversion to the intra-uterine state.

Hemingway diverges from the death instinct pattern in one significant way, however: whereas Freud notes that adults in conscious life try to reestablish the preshock condition and repress the traumatic experiences,[17] Hemingway actually works at reestablishing the shock condition itself. This is a vital distinction, of which every Freudian critic of Hemingway must be reminded.

Someone may ask, and justifiably, what are Hemingway's heroes trying to prove? Why does Harry Morgan have to demonstrate continually the measure of his cojones? Why don't the expatriates of *The Sun Also Rises* come back to the States and settle down? And Nick Adams? And Lt. Henry? And Robert Jordan? The answer is, they have seen real life, vital, authentic life, through the trauma of death, and they must continually recreate it. Catherine Henry appropriately alters the old quotation "The coward dies a thousand deaths, the brave but one" to "The brave dies perhaps two thousand deaths if he's intelligent." So Hemingway will not let his Leanders come to shore, but must constantly throw them back into the Hellespont.

And when there was no war for him to go to himself, Hemingway went to Spain, where for a nominal fee he could see death every afternoon in the bull ring. There is always much cruelty there, he wrote, and "there is always danger, either sought or unlooked for, and there is always death."

The only place where you could see life and death, *i.e.*, violent death now that the wars were over, was in the bull ring and I wanted very much to go to Spain where I could study it. I was trying to learn to write, commencing with the simplest things, and one of the simplest things of all and the most fundamental is violent death. It has none of the complications of death by disease, or so-called natural death, or the death of a friend or some one you have loved or have hated. . . .[18]

He sought the presence of violent death with a passion even more meaningful than that of Poe. He saw it as simple, fundamental, uncomplicated—and as a revealer of freedom.

The *barrera* seat is the nearest to the ring, where one can most effectively catch the movements of the bull and the emotions of the torero. "It is from the barrera that you see danger and learn to appreciate it." All of Hemingway's heroes are barrera-sitters. He is contemptuous of the tourists who come to bullfights merely to say they have been, then leave their expensive barrera seats after the first bull has been killed.

Because a truly good torero faces death frequently (a cowardly torero merely fakes the appearance of danger with body contortions), he becomes a symbol to Hemingway of one who really knows life. Describing a torero on the way to the arena, he speaks of him as "detached," the modifier he had previously used to describe the wounded veterans of "In Another Country";

There are some that smile and recognize friends on the ride, but nearly all are still-faced and detached. The matador, from living every day with death, becomes very detached, the measure of his detachment of course is the measure of his imagination and always on the day of the fight and finally during the whole end of the season, there is a detached something in their minds that you can almost see. What is there is death and you cannot deal in it each day and know each day there is a chance of receiving it without having it make a very plain mark. The banderilleros and the picadors are different. Their danger is relative. They are under orders; their responsibility is limited; and they do not kill.

This killing of the animals, and killing cleanly, is a much emphasized side of Hemingway's code. His delight in the bullfight, in fishing, in killing *kudu* in Africa, is all part of it. Actually, it has a psycho-philosophical basis. As Camus explains it, absolute freedom is the freedom to kill, to take life.[19] So when Romero says in *The Sun Also Rises* that he kills the bulls so they don't kill him, it is another way of saying that he asserts himself as an individual by *taking* life at the moment when he can most easily lose it.[20]

This does not mean that Hemingway is a wanton murderer at heart. Aesthetically and ethically, there is for him a vital distinction between the authentic individual who kills and the common man who slaughters.

The truly great killer must have a sense of honor and a sense of glory far beyond that of the ordinary bullfighter. In other words he must be a simpler man. . . . Killing cleanly and in a way which gives you aesthetic pleasure and pride has always been one of the greatest enjoyments of a part of the human race. Because the other part, which does not enjoy killing, has always been the more articulate and has furnished most of the good writers we have had a very few statements of the true enjoyment of killing. One of its greatest pleasures, aside from the purely aesthetic ones . . . is the feeling of rebellion against death which comes from its administering. Once you accept the rule of death thou shalt not kill is an easily and a naturally obeyed commandment. But when a man is still in rebellion against death he has pleasure in taking to himself one of the Godlike attributes; that of giving it. This is one of the most profound feelings in those men who enjoy killing.[21]

Taking to oneself this "Godlike attribute" is an integral part of a commonly held theory of the nontheistic existentialists: since there is no longer God, the true individual appropriates the deific qualities to himself. (This anthropocentric ethic will be discussed in a later chapter.)

Killing, as such, belongs to the acts of an individual. "Killing is not a feeling that you share," says Hemingway in his near-speechless elation after shooting a fine bull.[22] It maintains the subjectivism—the feeling that one directs the affairs of the earth from the Olympus of one's own will—that is the heart and core of existential living.

Speaking of the grand old bullfights of the past, before the bulls were bred down in size, length of horn, and natural strength, Hemingway says, "The whole end of the bullfight was the final sword thrust, the actual encounter between the man and the animal, what the Spanish call the moment of truth, and every move in the fight was to prepare the bull for that killing."[23] The "moment of truth" is the existential moment of anguish or dread crystallized into ritual—at the closest proximity to death, in the point-instant (to use Samuel Alexander's phrase) when the man is nearest in space and time to the horns of death, truth is revealed. Complications fall away at that moment—the question of existence is uppermost, for essence matters little beside survival—and things are at their simplest for the man facing down the saber to *la muerte.*

In a sense, the moment of truth is symbolic, and applies to the facing-death situations of all of Hemingway's heroes. For Nick, the moment of truth is the moment when he received the spine wound; for Jake, the moment when he was dealt futility in the groin; for Henry, when the mortar landed in his trench; and for Jordan, when the wall fell on him. The perpetual hero, reincarnated in each of these and other Hemingway characters, is kept vital as an individual by being cast continually into the teeth of death.

No one, of course, is more recognizable in the perpetual hero than the author himself, who grew up near the Indians in Michigan, went to war in Italy and to bullfights in Spain, who wrote about life in Paris, hunted bulls and lions in Africa, and went to war again in Spain. He has managed to keep his world alive, both in fiction and real life, by seeking death where it may be found most violent.

In 1944, he wrote a series of journalistic reports for *Collier's*, covering the invasion of Normandy, the *Blitzkrieg* in London, the taking of Paris, and the fighting in the Siegfried line. On invasion day, June 6, with his Zeiss fieldglasses wrapped in an old sock for protection, he rode an LCP through a machinegun-strafed, obstruction-mined surf in search of Fox Green Beach, carefully noting the danger and hauling aboard a soldier with a sizable wound in his lower abdomen. Three weeks later he was taking bomb-raids and belly-runs in the beautiful R.A.F. Tempests that were "sort of like a cross between Man o' War and Tallulah Bankhead in the best year either of them ever had." In November he was moving through the Schnee Eifel, where the Wump guns pock-marked the land twenty-four hours a day, watching the German SS troops stumbling out of grenaded fortifications, their faces black from concussion, bleeding at the nose and mouth, kneeling in muddy roads and clutching their stomachs. He described one German who had been kneeling in such a manner and was run over and mashed by a T.D.

"Mister Papa," as Malcolm Cowley says he was tagged by

the troops in Europe, has probably seen as much of life and death in their many forms as any ten ordinary men. But his philosophy of life has demanded it. The *ens realissimum* is possible only in the valley of the shadow of death, for it is there that man comes face to face with the uncanny feeling of *nada*. It is there, in the moment of truth, that the encrustations and accretions of historical man drop away, and the real, *ex-sisting* man emerges, timeless, Godlike, and free.

CHAPTER THREE

THE SIMPLE VERSUS THE COMPLICATED

WHAT HAPPENS when a boy goes off to war, experiences the moment of truth, and then comes back to his hometown, is the story of Hemingway's "Soldier's Home." Krebs, before he leaves, attends a Methodist school (accepted religion), belongs to a fraternity (accepted society), and wears "exactly the same height and style collar" (accepted fashion) as all his fraternity brothers. But war is death on patterns, and when Krebs returns he cannot tolerate them in any area of life.

He likes the looks of American girls, but "the world they were in was not the world he was in. He would like to have one of them. But it was not worth it. They were such a nice pattern." The slang they speak, the confectioneries where they hang out, the dance steps they dance, the protocol established for their dating, all form a complicated set of rules for anyone who has one of them. They live in "such a complicated world of already defined alliances and shifting feuds" that Krebs does not consider it worth the trouble to break into it.

This opposition between two worlds, one simple, the other complicated, is present in the entire body of Hemingway's fiction; and the bifurcation always occurs after an experience of violence or death, in which the distinction between authentic existence and complicated being is made clearly recognizable.

It is not just the girls that are too complicated for Krebs. "Here at home it was all too complicated." His mother wants him to be "really a credit to the community," like Charley Simmons—which involves complications like a steady job, marriage, and accepted religious activity. And when his mother finally appeals to him *as her son* to be like everybody else, he is attacked by nausea. "He had tried so to keep his life from being complicated."

Hemingway's distinction between the "simple" and the "complicated" is similar to the divisions made by many of the existentialists. It corresponds to the vital-comic antithesis of Kierkegaard, to the authentic-unauthentic of Heidegger, and to the sincerity-bad faith dialectic of Sartre.

"If existence really does precede essence," writes Sartre, "there is no explaining things away by reference to a fixed and given human nature. In other words, there is no determinism, man is free, man is freedom."[1] It is the basic nature of *every* man to be free—he is even "condemned to be free"—and it is this freedom that appears to him in the moment of anguish or dread. If he accepts his freedom and the responsibility it entails, he acts sincerely and authentically. If, however, he renounces his freedom in favor of the unresponsible, comfortable way, he acts in bad faith. Most people gladly have recourse to relative unconsciousness in order to escape the difficulties of the free life. The goal of bad faith is to put oneself out of reach.[2]

Most children automatically accept the universe as handed down to them and interpreted by the grown-ups, and many people never leave this infantile acceptance, or leave it only partially. These Simone de Beauvoir calls the "sub-men," because they voluntarily enslave themselves to facticity.[3] Women generally remain unauthentic. Mme. de Beauvoir's remarkable book *The Second Sex* has as its thesis the argument that since patriarchal times woman has been relegated to an *en-soi* or "object" position in human society, where man

reigns as *pour-soi* or "subject." The sexual act itself seems to
be the consummate symbol of this arrangement:

> Now, the woman lies in the posture of defeat; worse, the man
> rides her as he would an animal subject to bit and reins. She always
> feels passive: she *is* caressed, penetrated; she undergoes coition,
> where the man exerts himself actively. . . . She feels that she is an
> instrument: liberty rests wholly with the other.[4]

Another section of mankind that generally retreats into
irresponsibility is the religious. In Unamuno's *Abel Sanchez*,
Joaquin's wife hires a very religious girl as a maid. Joaquin
tries to stir her to anger, but she calmly turns his remarks
aside. Exasperated, he demands, "Why don't you rebel?"
"Rebel?" she replies, "I, sir? God and the Blessed Virgin
keep me from any rebellion, sir."

Sartre's Daniel, in *Les Chemins de la liberté,* also becomes
"religious" and refuses responsibility. He recognizes the possibility of his freedom when he is about to drown his cats and
realizes that he does not have to. For a long time, he is
tortured by the appeal of this freedom, by the need of
endorsing his own private existence. Sexually perverted, he
longs just to be, with no apologies: " 'Just *to be*,' he thinks.
'In the dark, at random! To be homo-sexual just as the oak is
oak.' "[5] He finds the responsibility of freedom too great to
bear alone, and effectually repudiates it by becoming a
religieux. He writes a long letter to Mathieu, describing the
conversion he experienced because he became aware of God's
seeing him and thereby constituting his existence:

> I used to long to become invisible, to go and leave no trace, on
> earth or in men's hearts. What anguish to discover that look as a
> universal medium from which I can't escape! But what a relief
> as well! I know at last that I am. I adopt for my own use, and to
> your disgust, your prophet's foolish wicked words: "I think, there-
> fore I am," which used to trouble me so sorely, for the more I

thought, the less I seemed to be; and I say, "I am seen, therefore I am." I need no longer bear the responsibility of my turbid and disintegrating self: he who sees me causes me to be; I am as he sees me.[6]

This shifting from the strenuous Cartesian premise to the less strenuous Berkeleian amounts, in the opinion of an existentialist, to a cowardly shuffling of responsibility off onto the idea of God. It is so distasteful to Mathieu that he wads up the letter and disgustedly tosses it out the train window. In his eyes, Daniel is no better than Charles, the invalid who thinks of himself as a stone because he is at the mercy of the "stand-ups," the nurses and doctors who take care of him.

For Kierkegaard, the failure to be one's self is the real "sickness unto death." A man who does not assert his own existence

forgets what his name is (in the divine understanding of it), does not dare to believe in himself, finds it too venturesome a thing to be himself, far easier and safer to be like the others, to become an imitation, a number, a cipher in the crowd.

This form of despair is hardly ever noticed in the world. Such a man, precisely by losing his self in this way, has gained perfectibility in adjusting himself to business, yea, in making a success in the world. Here there is no hindrance, no difficulty, occasioned by his self and his infinitization, he is ground smooth as a pebble, *courant* as a well-used coin. So far from being considered in despair, he is just what a man ought to be. In general the world has of course no understanding of what is truly dreadful. The despair which not only occasions no embarrassment but makes one's life easy and comfortable is naturally not regarded as despair. That this is the view of the world can also be seen in almost all the proverbs, which are merely rules for shrewd behavior.[7]

The idea that the average life is easy and comfortable is, of course, just what Sartre emphasizes in his illustration of the solicitous waiter, what Jaspers deplores in the *masse-Mensche,* and what Marcel attacks as the "functionalized" man.

Bad faith, then, is a concept common to the thinking of all the major existentialists, and means generally any acceptance of a way of living incognito, or of losing one's self in a larger entity, so as to slough off all personal responsibility for one's choices and actions.

There is a meaningful discussion related to this retreat into the identity of the group in Hemingway's short story, "The Gambler, the Nun, and the Radio." Some opiates of the people are mentioned: religion, music, economics, patriotism, sexual intercourse, drink, radio, gambling, ambition, belief in any new form of government, education, and bread ("the real actual opium of the people"). Each of these is a means of escape from the self. (The radio particularly figures in this story, since Frazer plays the radio softly all through the night to forget his pain.) Each is an avenue to the involved, self-forgetful, complicated way of life.

America, in Hemingway's opinion, is probably the most complicated land in the world. In a passage near the end of *Death in the Afternoon,* he makes clear his preference for the Spanish attitudes, which are much simpler than American attitudes because the Spanish continually contemplate death:

Someone with English blood has written: "Life is real; life is earnest, and the grave is not its goal." And where did they bury him? and what became of the reality and the earnestness? The people of Castile have great common sense. They could not produce a poet who would write a line like that. They know death is the unescapable reality, the one thing any man may be sure of; the only security; that it transcends all modern comforts and that with it you do not need a bathtub in every American home, nor, when you have it, do you need the radio.

The bullfight is the symbol of the contrast between the English and the Spanish: the English do not like the sight of death, which alone reduces life to simple terms. It was his preference for other, less complicated countries—for France and Spain in *The Sun Also Rises,* for the dark continent in *Green Hills of*

Africa, and for Italy in *Across the River and into the Trees*—
that drew upon Hemingway the scorn of American critics like
Geismar.[8]

The "complicated" lives of the husband and wife in "Mr.
and Mrs. Elliot," a story which in respect to satire might have
been written by Sinclair Lewis, express Hemingway's opinion
of many Americans. Both come to marriage in middle age from
rather puritanical backgrounds—he has been a Harvard man
and a poet, and she has been the proprietress of a tea shop.
For a while they try to have a baby, a situation made more
revealing by the information that he masturbated on the night
of the wedding. Finally they settle into a pattern of quiet life,
with their tea at fixed hours, with no more intercourse, no
violence, and—no fertility. It is the picture of a real waste
land, peopled with hollow men. One might even wonder if
the title expresses an oblique reference to the poet of *The
Waste Land.*

A great deal of fun is made, too, of the naïve American in
"Canary for One," where an exceedingly provincial lady
tourist from the States meets on a train a pair of Americans
residing in France. She has forbidden her daughter to marry
a Swiss engineering student because "Americans make the
best husbands," and she repeats several times to the American
couple that she is glad they are married to each other because
"Americans make the best husbands"—it is her favorite plati-
tude. The story ends with an O. Henry denouement: "We were
returning to Paris to set up separate residences." The American
lady with the canary (which she doubtless expects to replace
the Swiss lad in her daughter's affections) leads a formulated
life, telling her bigotries for beads. Whenever the train stops,
she always hovers near it for fear she will be left behind,
breaking the pattern of her trip. Her travelling is handled for
her by Cook's, and her name is in a sheaf of others in the Cook
agent's pocket. She is one of Kierkegaard's "ciphers."

Similar contempt is heaped on the American tourist who
stares at Cantwell and Renata in the Gritti dining room in

Across the River and into the Trees. He sees nothing of
Venice that is not in Baedeker. Baedeker is even once referred
to as his Lady.

Even the tourists who go to bullfights go simply to say that
they have been. Early in the afternoon they desert their
expensive barrera seats, which are then taken over by the
Spaniards, who really want to see death. In *The Sun Also
Rises,* when he is discussing *afición* and the *aficionado* with
the Spanish hotel manager, Jake Barnes thinks, "Somehow it
was taken for granted that an American could not have
afición. He might simulate it or confuse it with excitement,
but he could not really have it." The influx of "compassionate"
American tourists, says Hemingway, even led to the "protec-
tive" covering of the horses used in the ring. Actually the
covers protect nothing, but merely conceal the horses' injuries
from the eyes of the complicated patrons who like to veil
suffering.[9]

The truly expatriated American, of course, is different. He
is like a man without a country, his existence sheared of
complication even to the extent of abandoning his father-
land. But the expatriation must be spiritual as well as geo-
graphical. A mere transplanted residence is not necessarily
equal to simplification.

The contrast between the authentic Hemingway hero and
the complicated, merely transplanted American is evident
between Jake Barnes and Robert Cohn of *The Sun Also Rises*
or between Richard Cantwell and the orderly Jackson in
Across the River and into the Trees. Jake, as a result of his
wound, leads a simple, unentangled life—he is Jake Barnes,
no more, no less. Cohn, on the other hand, is forever strug-
gling to be something other than himself. His emotions
bind him first to Frances, then to Brett Ashley. He wants to
go to South America, but Frances doesn't want to go. Jake
says, "Tell her to go to hell." "I can't," says Cohn. "I have
certain obligations to her." When Jake walks down the
Boulevard Raspail, he thinks:

It is a street I do not mind walking down at all. But I cannot stand to ride along it. Perhaps I had read something about it once. That was the way Robert Cohn was about all of Paris. Possibly from Mencken. Mencken hates Paris, I believe. So many young men get their likes and dislikes from Mencken.

Cohn is thus grouped with those who get their opinions from others, and conformism is an unpardonable offense to the true existentialist. It is somewhat ironic that Hemingway's fictive world was to become a pattern of behavior for many young people, just as Mencken's pose already had.

Cantwell is symbolically alone in a duck blind both at the first and near the end of the book in which he appears. He contrasts quite obviously with the orderly who drives him to Venice. While he is facing death from a bad heart muscle and is making the most of his last visit to the beloved city, Jackson reads comic books and sleeps. When Cantwell directs him to take an unmapped road to Venice, Jackson complains, "I don't trust those side roads in this low country." Cantwell gets out, inspects the road, returns to the car and says to quit worrying, it's a boulevard. After a moment he adds, "Say, Jackson, do you always suffer so much any time you go off a highway onto a secondary road?" Jackson, of course, always prefers the conventional way, the well-mapped way, to the way of the adventurous individualist. He is like the American lady in "Canary for One."

Cantwell invites him to the duck-shoot, but he would rather "stay in that sack." When Cantwell returns, he is told that his driver is asleep. "He would be," says the Colonel. Cantwell asks the Barone if Jackson has eaten. "Eaten and slept and eaten and slept," is the reply. "He has also read a little in some illustrated books he brought with him." "Comic books," the Colonel says.

The Colonel has been made an existentialist by the war and death he has seen. His life is marvellously uncomplicated, even by the past. On the way to Venice he stops the driver, determines by triangulation where it was that he had been

wounded thirty years before, and, squatting low, relieves
himself in the exact spot. To complete the monument, he digs
a hole with his knife and inserts a 10,000-lira note and tamps
the earth back. "That is twenty years at 500 lira a year for
the Medaglia d'Argento al Valore Militare. The V.C. carries
ten guineas, I believe. The D.S.C. is non-productive. The
Silver Star is free. I'll keep the change." He is ritually dis-
charging himself from the past, adorning the resting place
of the Cantwell who died on the spot thirty years earlier. "A
poor effort," he says when he has relieved himself. "But my
own."

At the end of the story, he dies in the back of his car after
handing a note to Jackson instructing him to see that some
properties are returned to their owners. The final sentence of
the book is: " 'They'll return them all right, through channels,'
Jackson thought, and put the car in gear." "Through channels"
—complications which stand for the unauthentic, for Jackson,
for the uninitiated, those who have not felt the castigating
wound, all of which Cantwell's life opposed. But now he is
dead and quit for tomorrow.

There is little doubt that this battle-hardened old individualist is, to a considerable extent, Hemingway himself, although
the latter disavows any connection. Cantwell calls Renata
"Daughter," refers to himself as "slug-nutty," has a bad leg,
has been married to a female journalist, drinks a lot, has a
keen sense of smell, and is Hemingway's age (51) at the time
of publication of the novel. The title phrase is from Stonewall
Jackson's reported last words,[10] and the book may be Hemingway's farewell lest his repeated flirtations with death end all
his writing and he leave no final word about himself.

John Peale Bishop, in his famous article "The Missing All,"
struck the key that explains Cantwell's—or Hemingway's—
rigorous simplicity and individualism:

It was his awareness of death that separated Hemingway from the
Middle West. The West had never known what the war was about;
Hemingway returned from it like Krebs in that story which is the

best account written by an American of the returned soldier. Krebs found all communication with his family impossible. He sat on the front porch and saw the girls that walked on the other side of the street. "He liked the look of them much better than the French or German girls. But the world they were in was not the world he was in."[11]

Hemingway's own isolation is seen quite directly in *Green Hills of Africa*, which is definitely autobiographical. There he says, referring to the tattoos of the natives, "The tribal marks and the tattooed places seemed natural and handsome adornments and I regretted not having any of my own. My own scars were all informal." His scars are not the marks of society or of any "complicated" group; they are rather the evidences of his remarkable individuality, unsystematically collected as the mementoes of the times he has faced the moment of truth.

One evening after a highly successful hunt with the Wanderobo-Masai, Hemingway, Kamau, Garrick, M'Cola and the others sat down to a meal of Grant-gazelle tenderloin and German beer. Hemingway was sitting on a petrol box with his back against the tree. But—

It seemed too complicated sitting on a petrol case and I spread my raincoat on the ground in front of the fire where the ground had been dried by the heat and stretched my legs out, leaning my back against the wooden case.

Now in the usual sense of the word, there seems to be nothing more simple than sitting on a petrol case with one's back against a tree. In view of Hemingway's repeated use of the word, though, it seems that what he means is that people who lead complicated lives—in religion, Rotary clubs, tribal tattoos, regimental discipline—would sit that way, and Hemingway, who eschews complications, moves to the ground to sprawl more individually, more personally, more *ex-sistentially*.

The convenient bisection of life into the simple and the

complicated is also a key to understanding Hemingway's
feelings about women. He entitled one volume of short stories
Men Without Women, and he is consistent throughout his
fiction in the attitude that his men are at their finest when
they are without women. He seems to feel, as Berdyaev wrote
of Dostoievski's women, that "woman is a stumbling-block in
the way of male destiny."[12] Edmund Wilson was correct in
saying that the only women with whom Nick Adams (*i.e.,*
Nick Adams as he is traced through the entire development
of the Hemingway hero) ever has satisfactory relations are
the little Indian girls, because they are of a lower caste and
he can get rid of them easily.[13] All the other women threaten
complication.

Nick has to break with Marjorie in "The End of Something"
because their love has settled into the complicated way, with
her *savoir-faire* tending to her possessing him.

> "There's going to be a moon tonight," said Nick. . . .
> "I know it," Marjorie said happily.
> "You know everything," Nick said. . . . "You do. You know
> everything. That's the trouble. You know you do."

The trouble was that she knew everything—he had taught her
—and now it had become fixed, a pattern, and he had to
break away.

Bill and Nick continue the subject in "The Three-Day Blow."
Bill says, "Once a man's married he's absolutely bitched. . . .
He hasn't got anything more. Nothing. Not a damn thing.
He's done for. . . ." And then he discusses the complications
of family life and the Sunday visits a husband must make to
please his wife. Nick knows that *if he chooses* he can revive
the affair and go into town Saturday night. "It was a good
thing to have in reserve." But the important thing is that
he is free to choose.[14]

The tragedy of wasted talent in "The Snows of Kilimanjaro"
began with Harry's first marriage and became intensified with

each succeeding marriage. Actually it was the luxury his
wives brought him that ruined him, not the wives themselves;
surrounded by the costlier things of life, he had neglected to
write. Now he had returned to Africa to "work the fat off his
soul," and he was camping in the shadow of the mountain
with the Ngàje Ngài—the house of God, the symbol of
perfection—at its summit. But he, like the leopard, had been
frozen in the ascent, his development arrested by the accretion
of luxury.

Hemingway took up the question of luxury again in *To Have
and Have Not*, which some reviewers hailed as a piece of
socialistic-economic propaganda. It is probably only a coin-
cidence, but this book appeared just two years after the
publication of Gabriel Marcel's *Être et avoir* (1935), in which
Marcel made a distinction between *having*, which implies
possession that can be objectified, and *being*, which is freedom
from encumbrance. In other words, having is a burden which
makes it more difficult for being to exist. A similar contrast is
dramatically clear when the body of Harry Morgan, a "have-
not" who died shipping gun-runners because he had to feed
his family, is carried back through the moonlit harbor, passing
among the yachts of the "haves," who lead empty, meaningless
lives by day and then take luminal to sleep by night. Posses-
sions are fat on the soul: they complicate life.[15] Here is a new
secular asceticism.

Francis Macomber's life was complicated by marriage to a
dominant woman, and it was his awakening, his beginning to
ex-sist, that demanded of her possessive complex that she shoot
him lest she lose him. From the beginning of the story, he is
a complicated man, a coward, one of the "messy." Two telling
phrases from his lips in the first hundred words are "I suppose
it's the thing to do" and "What ought I to give them?" both
concerned with convention as the world sees it. But he doesn't
know the hero-conventions, like not asking a professional
hunter not to carry back tales of cowardice.

His new birth apparently starts during the two hours he

lies awake waiting for Margot to return from Wilson's tent. When she does return, he says, "You think that I'll take anything."

"I know you will, sweet."

"Well, I won't."

Perhaps he has the existential nausea, the feeling of nothingness that precedes the establishment of the fundamental self —everything is gone, so what the hell.

Therefore when it is necessary on the following day to go in after a wounded buffalo bull, he feels not fear but elation. He has become, in Wilson's words, "a ruddy fire-eater." He experiences "a wild unreasonable happiness that he had never known before." "You know," he says to Wilson, "I don't think I'd ever be afraid of anything again. Something happened in me after we saw the buff and started after him. Like a dam bursting. It was pure excitement. . . . I feel absolutely different."

The title "The Short Happy Life of Francis Macomber" now assumes meaning. True life, genuine existence, has begun for him. It had its birth pangs the night before when he waited for Margot in the darkness; and the Freudian implication of the dam bursting is of fertility, of sudden vitality where before there was only sterility.

As Macomber is reborn, Wilson becomes a spectator instead of the strong character of the story. He

had seen men come of age before and it always moved him. It was not a matter of their twenty-first birthday. . . . It's that some of them stay little boys so long, Wilson thought. Sometimes all their lives. Their figures stay boyish when they're fifty. The great American boy-men. . . . He'd seen it in the war work the same way.

He anticipates that Macomber's new attitude will mean the end of his cuckoldry. Immediately after Macomber suggested going in after the buffalo quickly, Margot had turned white, and had gone to sit in the shade. Wilson could tell by the way she talked that she was "very afraid of something." After she has shot Macomber, Wilson remarks, "That was a pretty thing to do. He *would* have left you too." The short, happy life had come into true *ex-sistence* during the night, and the courage before the buffalo had confirmed it. Margot had lost him; so she shot him.

An existential interpretation will likewise answer the question of why Catherine Henry had to die in *A Farewell to Arms*.

Catherine is one of the most likely of Hemingway's women to make a Hemingway man happy and give him a maximum amount of freedom. Throughout the novel in which she appears, she is amenable to Henry's suggestions, eager to please him. She too is simple, perhaps because she is a war nurse and has herself seen much death and brutality. In the questionable hotel in Milan—the one with the red plush furnishings which made Catherine feel like a whore for seven minutes —Henry says, "You're a fine simple girl."

"I am a simple girl," she replies. "No one ever understood it except you. . . . I'm a very simple girl."

"I didn't think so at first," says Henry. "I thought you were a crazy girl."

"I was a little crazy. But I wasn't crazy in any complicated manner."

Yet from the beginning there is a hint of complication in their alliance. When Henry, having hardly gotten to know her, invites Rinaldi to come in to see her, Rinaldi refuses, explaining that he prefers "the simpler pleasures." The simpler pleasures are those of the whorehouse, where a man pays a fee but does not become entangled. And even after Henry's farewell to arms, which harks the reader back to Nick Adams' "separate peace," he is still not, like Nick, free from a lingering feeling of guilt:

The war was a long way away. Maybe there wasn't any war. There was no war here. Then I realized it was over for me. But I did not have the feeling that it was really over. I had the feeling of a boy who thinks of what is happening at a certain hour at the schoolhouse from which he has played truant.

It is only when the complication is intensified by the presence of Catherine and their removal to the Swiss chalet that he ceases to feel compunctions about his truancy.

The extreme complication, however, the one demanding death for both the mother and the baby, is the baby itself. It is evident that the duties of fatherhood will threaten Henry's freedom. Catherine asks him, after telling him that she is pregnant, if he feels trapped. "Maybe a little," he answers. "But not by you."

"I didn't mean by me," she says. "You mustn't be stupid. I meant trapped at all."

Henry says, "You always feel trapped biologically."

The idea is not new here in Hemingway; in fact, it seems ingrained in his thinking. He, too, had come not too happily to fatherhood. And the hand of the author is unmistakable in "Cross-Country Snow," where Nick regrets that he must relinquish his skiing in the Alps with a male companion to return to the States for his wife to have a baby.

Catherine regrets the coming birth of the child, because she realizes the psychological constriction it puts upon Henry. More than once she apologizes for making trouble for him. He behaves more gracefully *in situation*, however, than the male in "Hills Like White Elephants," who wants his sweetheart to have an abortion so that they can go on as they have lived in the past, or than Richard Gordon in *To Have and Have Not*, who took his wife to "that dirty aborting horror," or than Mathieu in Sartre's *Age of Reason*, who planned, until Daniel offered to marry her, to have an abortion performed on Marcelle.

But the darkness of Catherine's death is a cloud spread by the author as a disguise for pulling off a *deus ex machina* to save his hero from the existential hell of a complicated life. Henry's philippic against the impersonal "they" that kills you —that killed Aymo gratuitously, that gave Rinaldi the syphilis, and that now is killing Catherine—is fine rhetoric and perhaps much in place for a universe without God in our time, but it is the author himself who is guilty of Catherine's death because of his fondness for the hero, and who makes a scapegoat of the world. The Henry who walks off into the rainy night at the end of *A Farewell to Arms* is like the Orestes who exits with the Furies in *Les Mouches*—he is alone, tormented, but very much alive in an existential sense.[16]

Several critics have noted the recurrence of rain (or other forms of precipitation) in Hemingway's fiction, and especially in *A Farewell to Arms,* as a harbinger of disaster.[17] Since it *is* connected with death, they generally agree that this function is diametrically opposite that of the precipitation symbol in the wasteland world of T. S. Eliot. But I believe that the rain is a symbol of fertility in Hemingway, too, though in a slightly different sense than in Eliot. To Hemingway death means rebirth for the existentialist hero in its presence, and therefore the rain, as an omen of death, at the same time predicts rebirth. The precipitation-death-rebirth combination is especially pertinent to the recurrent use of rain in *A Farewell to Arms* and of snow in *For Whom the Bell Tolls;* and a case might even be made for a theory that old Santiago, who is an existentialist in the grand style ("He was too simple to wonder when he had attained humility"), is an authentic individual because he is an old man *of the sea,* which is both a perennial reminder of man's finitude and a primordial womb symbol.

The striving for simplicity, what Jaspers calls the "drive toward honesty" or the "drive toward the basic,"[18] applies also to writing. Even words can become too complicated to suit Hemingway. His prose style was doubtless influenced by his journalistic training,[19] by writers like Stephen Crane and Mark Twain, by association with Gertrude Stein, and by his reading in the Bible, where he must have found the trick of the repetitive "he said." But it is possible that his use of simple vocabulary and syntax may stem at least partly from his distrust of the complicated in any form, even in language. His preference for the concrete is evident in *Death in the Afternoon,* where he tells the old lady he has been "talking horseshit," and defines it as "the term now to describe unsoundness in an abstract conversation or, indeed, any over-metaphysical tendency in speech." In *A Farewell to Arms* there is the celebrated passage:

There were many words that you could not stand to hear and finally only the names of places had dignity. Certain numbers were the same way and certain dates and these with the names of the places were all you could say and have them mean anything. Abstract words such as glory, honor, courage, or hallow were obscene beside the concrete names of villages, the numbers of roads, the names of rivers, the numbers of regiments and the dates.[20]

This is existential sentiment, emphasizing the very real kinship between the philosophy of existence and the science of phenomenology: value is only in living, not in abstractions, and concrete places and people are meaningful because we determine our selves in relation to the things around us. Glory, honor, courage and sanctity are conceptions of a "complicated" ethics.

Sartre has said that the writer's job is to cure the "sick" language that is incommunicative.[21] Iris Murdoch, in attempting to answer what the sickness of the language really is, says it is the fact that we can no longer take language for granted as a medium of communication. "Its transparency has gone. We are like people who for a long time looked out of a window without noticing the glass—and then one day began to notice this too."[22]

Hemingway also feels this way. Our time demands a simple prose, with an Eliot-like emphasis on semantics. The author of *Death in the Afternoon* lectures to the old lady on the skill that should be employed in the use of every word. The word in illustration being "decadence," Hemingway concludes, "So you see, madame, we must be careful chucking the term decadence about since it cannot mean the same to all who read it."

And this exacting use of his words should emphasize

clearly the seriousness with which Hemingway repeatedly
employs the contrasting terms *simple* and *complicated.*

For certain of the existentialists, the philosophical tension
of the subjective-objective dialectic (represented for Hemingway by the simple and the complicated) is the *absurd.*
Absurdity is the word used by Kierkegaard to represent the
state of being which is peculiar to the knight of faith: the
knight lays hold of the absurd as the only thing that can save
him.[23] Camus, who treats the idea at more length in *The Myth
of Sisyphus,* illustrates it with the picture of a man armed
only with a sword attacking men armed with machineguns.
What makes this situation absurd is neither the sword nor the
machineguns, but the juxtaposition of the two, the absurd
combination. Similarly, man is not absurd, nor is the objective
world, but place man over against the world and the absurdity,
the tension between the subjective and objective natures,
arises. The authentic individual lives in the absurd, maintain-
ing the tension throughout every act and hour of his existence.
"Living is keeping the absurd alive."[24]

This viewpoint provides the recitative for Sartre's famous
early novel, *La Nausée.* M. Antoine Roquentin, who has lived
with the emotion of absurdity for a long time, at last discovers
what it really is while standing in a garden and looking at the
root of a chestnut tree: absurdity is the distance between him
and the root. At last! he exclaims, I have found the key to
existence, the key to my nausea, to my own life!

The fact that he who lives in perpetual recognition of the
absurd is subject to the natural psychosomatic phenomenon of
nausea is worth noting, for it is common to the characters of
both Sartre and Hemingway. Nausea is Roquentin's usual
state (*mon état normal*). He repeatedly exhibits a passion for
the viscous, even for his own saliva; he can stand mesmerized
for minutes by the sight of his spittle inching toward the drain
in a sink. I believe this abhorrent obsession is explanable as
Sartre's attempt to represent by the viscous the distance between solid and liquid, making it a symbol of the object-

subject dialectic; it stands for absurdity, for tension, and for Sartre's whole *en-soi-pour-soi* phenomenology.

If it is true that, for Hemingway, violence reveals the absurd (*i.e.*, the simplification-complication dialectic), it is likewise true that the feeling of nausea begins to accompany violence as early as the Indian camp episode of Nick Adams, in which the trauma he experiences coming away from the Indian tent where a baby was delivered with a jack-knife while its father slit his throat with a razor is an expressed contrast with the joy he had felt over the pastoral scenery as he first came up.

Nick feels the nausea again when he almost shoots his father for making him wear his father's old underwear (in "Fathers and Sons") and again when he sees the ex-pugilist's ears in "The Battler," which represents the violence of the fight game. And even where there is no violence, but instead a feeling of dread at the threat of impending complications, there is the experience of nausea, as in "A Very Short Story," where Nick narrowly escapes the complications of a legal marriage and forced return to the States.

Krebs has a similar experience of nausea in "Soldier's Home," where it is produced by the contrast between the fundamental simplicity he has met in the war and the threatening complications he faces after the war. He feels it when he has to lie like an old soldier, and he feels it when his mother appeals to him as her son to settle down into a routine way of life—he is literally sick at the thought.

Chapter VI of *In Our Time* is the sketch of a bullfighter who kills five bulls in one afternoon. He gets through the first couple very well. But as soon as the fifth one has taken the sword, he retches violently—and the moment of truth is thus linked with nausea.

Nausea accompanies, or perhaps is responsible for, William Campbell's realization of freedom in "A Pursuit Race." Campbell is the advance man for a burlesque show, and his life strikes him as one long pursuit race, trying to stay ahead of the show. But at last the morning comes when he adopts

the I-care-not attitude which the reduction from complication
to simplicity brings (cf. Hemingway's Shakespearean talisman,
"By my troth, I care not"), and stays in bed. He is nauseated,
but he has decided to be free of the complicated pursuit race.

The whole story of Harry Morgan's life in *To Have and
Have Not* is measured out in acts of violence and fits of nausea.
Very early in the book he is a witness to the machinegunning
of three Cubans as they leave the bar where they and Harry
have had a drink together. An ice-wagon horse is hit by a stray
bullet and goes down in the harness; the other horse plunges
wildly, only to become enmeshed in the lines. When old
Pancho tries to stop the killers, the Negro takes a shotgun and
blows the old man's head into a hundred pieces. As Harry
Morgan sparely puts it, "The whole thing made me feel pretty
bad." Later, when one one of the Cuban revolutionaries shoots
his friend Albert, Harry again feels sick inside, even though
he himself had contemplated killing Albert to keep him from
talking to the authorities about what the boat was used for.
And after he kills the Cubans and is shot doing it, he feels his
strength draining away in "a steady faint nausea."

A similar nausea precedes the death of El Sordo in *For
Whom the Bell Tolls*. He and his guerrillas are surrounded by
the Fascists on a hilltop, waiting for the planes that will drop
the explosive death upon them. Sordo is wounded, death is
imminent, and nausea is natural.

All of these instances of nausea occur rather casually in
Hemingway's fiction, scattered between "Indian Camp" and
Santiago's abdominal nervousness in *The Old Man and the Sea*.
Each appears quite natural under the circumstances sur-
rounding it, and a panoramic view of all that Hemingway has
written is necessary to see the importance of the pattern.

In one passage only, where the connection between death
and nausea is prolonged over an intense several pages, is this
not true. That is Pilar's beautifully macabre account of "the
smell of death." Pilar says she could smell death when she
was near Kashkin, the dynamiter whom Jordan replaced.

Jordan cannot believe it; perhaps it was the smell of fear. *"De la muerte,"* insists Pilar. She proceeds to describe the smell. Part of it is

". . . the smell that comes when, on a ship, there is a storm and the portholes are closed up. Put your nose against the brass handle of a screwed-tight porthole on a rolling ship that is swaying under you so that you are faint and hollow in the stomach and you have a part of that smell. . . .

"After that of the ship you must go down the hill in Madrid to the Puente de Toledo early in the morning to the *matadero* and stand there on the wet paving when there is a fog from the Manzanares and wait for the old women who go before daylight to drink the blood of the beasts that are slaughtered. When such an old woman comes out of the *matadero,* holding her shawl around her, with her face gray and her eyes hollow, and the whiskers of age on her chin, and on her cheeks, set in the waxen white of her face as the sprouts grow from the seed of a bean, not bristles, but pale sprouts in the death of her face; put your arms around her tight, *Inglés,* and hold her to you and kiss her on the mouth and you will know the second part that odor is made of. . . .

"Kiss one, *Inglés,* for thy knowledge's sake and then, with this in thy nostrils, walk back up into the city and when thou seest a refuse pail with dead flowers in it plunge thy nose deep into it and inhale so that no scent mixes with those thou hast already in thy nasal passages."

"Now have I done it," Robert Jordan said. "What flowers were they?"

"Chrysanthemums."

"Continue," Robert Jordan said. "I smell them."

"Then," Pilar went on, "it is important that the day be in autumn with rain or at least some fog, or early winter even and now thou shouldst continue to walk through the city and down the Calle de Salud smelling what thou wilt smell where they are sweeping out the *casas de putas* and emptying the slop jars into the drains and, with this odor of love's labor lost mixed sweetly with soapy water and cigarette butts only faintly reaching thy nostrils, thou shouldst go on to the Jardin Botanico where at night those girls who can no longer work in the houses do their work

against the iron gates of the park and the iron picketed fences and
upon the sidewalks. It is there in the shadow of the trees against
the iron railings that they will perform all that a man wishes from
the simplest requests at a remuneration of ten centimes up to a
peseta for that great act that we are born to and there, on a dead
flower bed that has not yet been plucked out and replanted, and so
serves to soften the earth that is so much softer than the sidewalk,
thou wilt find an abandoned gunny sack with the odor of the wet
earth, the dead flowers, and the doings of that night. In this sack
will be contained the essence of it all, both the dead earth and the
dead stalks of the flowers and their rotted blooms and the smell
that is both the death and birth of man. Thou wilt wrap this sack
around thy head and try to breathe through it."

"No."

"Yes," Pilar said. "Thou wilt wrap this sack around thy head and
try to breathe and then, if thou hast not lost any of the previous
odors, when thou inhalest deeply, thou wilt smell the odor of
death-to-come as we know it."

To many readers this doubtless seems like a pornographic
caricature of Edgar Allan Poe or Ambrose Bierce, or even
Émile Zola. But it is an authentic psychological cathartic
for reducing life to its simplest terms. "The odor of death-to-
come" is not really very different from the feeling of dread
or nausea belonging to the man who in Heidegger's philosophy
runs forward to death, who in Sartre stands poised on the
brink of a cliff, and who in Jaspers has travelled much within
himself and has discovered death to be one of his boundaries.
In the moment of nausea the human mind in the human body
at the instant of psychosomatic spasm sloughs off every care
but that of survival, or simple existence, establishing the
existentialist's favorite maxim: "Existence is prior to essence."
Nausea is a physical manifestation of the moment of truth, the
most revealing symbol of the bifurcation between the authentic
and the unauthentic, the *pour-soi* and the *en-soi*, the absurd
and the common, or, as Hemingway has put it, between the
simple and the complicated.

CHAPTER FOUR

THE DEATH
OF THE GODS

"DEAD ARE ALL GODS," sang Nietzsche's Zarathustra.
"Now will we that the Superman live!"[1]
Zarathustra was a kind of contemporary Christ. He too
was thirty years old when he left home to begin his liberating
mission; he too sought to make men free from the past; he
too was to have but a small band of real followers; and he too
was in a sense crucified by the world. He was the Christ who
came to save men from God in the nineteenth century.

For years Nietzsche was roundly condemned as an atheist
and a detractor and a neo-pagan. But then it was gradually
understood that he did not kill God, but merely preached his
funeral after having found him dead in the hearts and lives
of his contemporaries.[2] God for him, like God for Heidegger,
was just no longer meaningful to human affairs. Religion had
become religiosity, and the church had become a sacerdotal
instrument for teaching a kind of morality which set up the
priest as the highest type of human being.

It is all a holy lie! cried Nietzsche. The God who punishes
and rewards, the afterlife, the conscience of man understood
as the knowledge that good and evil are permanent values,
morality as the denial of all natural processes, truth as given,

revealed, and identified with the teaching of the priests: it is all a holy lie invented to enslave mankind!

The same sentiment appeared with much pathos in the world of Dostoievski. It gleams especially from a memorable jewel set into *The Brothers Karamazov,* "The Grand Inquisitor." In that remarkable tale, Christ comes back to walk the streets of Seville, reaching forth his hands to heal the multitudes. But the old Cardinal, the Grand Inquisitor, orders his imprisonment. In the secrecy of a cell they meet, and the old churchman accuses him of wreaking havoc upon the people by reappearing. "Thou hast no right," he reproaches, "to add anything to what Thou hadst said of old." At last the Prisoner approaches the Cardinal and softly kisses his bloodless old lips.

> That was all his answer. The old man shuddered. His lips moved. He went to the door, opened it, and said to Him: "Go, and come no more. . . . come not at all, never, never!" And he let Him out into the dark alleys of the town. The Prisoner went away.

Alyosha guesses the secret of Ivan's terrible Cardinal: he does not believe in God! His has never been the burning personal experience of the *Shekinah,* the presence of the living God, such as Moses had, and David, and Isaiah, and Jesus, and Augustine. Even if he had experienced the soul-twisting *Anfechtung* of Luther, he had not arrived at the knowledge of God. Christianity, for him, was tantamount to the social order, no more, no less. It satisfied the people. It preserved the status quo. It gratified the priesthood. Therefore it deserved to exist.

But therefore, for Dostoievski and for Nietzsche, it did *not* deserve to exist, and it would not exist. They had their thumbs upon the pulse of the time. All men would soon rebel against the kind of God they formerly created and worshipped. "As soon as men have all of them denied God," says the Devil in Ivan Karamazov's nightmare, "—and I believe

that period, analogous with geological periods, will come to
pass—the old conception of the universe will fall of itself without cannibalism and what's more the old morality, and everything will begin anew. Men will unite to take from life all it
can give, but only for joy and happiness in the present world.
Man will be lifted up with a spirit of divine Titanic pride
and the man-god will appear." The "man-god." So Nietzsche
preached the Superman. "Surmount" became his watchword
—*Überwinden!* Surmount the pale and bloodless man of today,
become the Superman! It was "the latter-day humanistic
evangel" to replace the intellectual slavery of contemporary
Christianity and the bland offerings of Hegelianism. As one
writer has said, Nietzsche "spent himself in the attempt to
make a godless world a human and hopeful one, in which man
would regain rank and value."[3]

These two pronouncements, of the disappearance of God
and the resurgence of human value, have become the foci
of the ellipse described by the movement of a great body of
literature in our time. There have been many disciples to
preach this new humanistic gospel in the twentieth century.
Among them is Albert Camus, who denies the justification for
Kierkegaard's leap from the crest of dread to the being of God,
and claims that integrity lies in being able to remain on the
dizzying crest.[4] Among them is Sartre, who makes a sort of
Zarathustra out of Orestes when he repudiates Zeus in *Les
Mouches*, who avers in *Huis Clos* that hell is other people, who
intimates in *Le Sursis* that God is merely a respectable term for
the anonymity sought by those who prefer the *en-soi* to the
pour-soi, and who is avowedly an atheist throughout the seven-
hundred-odd pages of his major work, *L'Être et le néant*.
Among them is Franz Kafka, whose surveyor K. in *The Castle*
is estranged from the townspeople because he knows God
(either Count Westwest or the castle itself) is dead, even
though the colossal impact of this news has not yet penetrated
to the minds of those who are nearest the castle.[5]

And among them too is Hemingway, who seems to feel

that the disappearance of God is one of the factors that make our times so different and so difficult.

"*Are you croyant?*" asks the nonagenarian Count Greffi of Lt. Henry in *A Farewell to Arms.*

"At night," replies Henry.

"Perhaps I have outlived my religious feeling," continues the Count after an interval of billiards.

"My own comes only at night," says Henry.

Only at night do Hemingway's men and women feel the vestiges of religion, for it is only at night that the mind is not well lighted and well ordered. As Jake Barnes says about his ability to forget Brett Ashley, "It is awfully easy to be hard-boiled about everything in the daytime, but at night it is another thing." At night, the mind is susceptible to what Jung would have called the collective memory of a religious past.

This day-and-night, light-and-dark symbolism cuts a wide swathe through Hemingway's fiction. Its most dramatic statement, of course, is in the little *nada*-story "A Clean, Well-Lighted Place," with the clean, well-lighted place representing all that is utterly reduced to simplicity—no noise, no customers, and an old man with no wife to go home to. It is apparent in "Big Two-Hearted River," where Nick disdains fishing in the darker recesses of the stream. It is recalled by the title *Death in the Afternoon,* since the real toreros, who actually repeat the moment ot truth, fight only in the afternoon, while the aesthetically and ethically cheaper fighters take night billing. It shows up again and again in the thinking of the characters, as in Jake Barnes, who says, "There is no reason why because it is dark you should look at things differently from when it is light. The hell there isn't!" Or as in Philip Rawlings, who vows at night to love and marry Dorothy, but, when she asks him about it the next morning, thunders, "Never believe what I say at night. I lie like hell at night."[6]

Religion, then, belongs principally among the night thoughts. So old Anselmo can say in the daytime that "we do not have God here anymore, neither His Son nor the Holy Ghost."

But when he sees the Fascist cavalry unit ride by in the twilight with Sordo's gun and a strange blanket roll lashed down like a pea pod with bulges beneath the ropes, and when he crosses Sordo's hilltop and sees the bomb-craters and understands that the blanket roll contained the heads of Sordo and his men, he walks along in the dark freezing with fear, and begins to pray for the souls of Sordo and his band. "It was the first time he had prayed since the start of the movement." And it was at night.

In *The Sun Also Rises,* Jake Barnes enters a church to say prayers, but the suspicion of any religious affirmation is soon dashed to pieces. The very quality of Jake's prayer in the cathedral (he says he is "technically" a Catholic) points up the inefficacy of supernatural communication in our time:

I knelt and started to pray and prayed for everybody I thought of, Brett and Mike and Bill and Robert Cohn and myself, and all the bullfighters, separately for the ones I liked, and lumping all the rest, then I prayed for myself again, and while I was praying for myself I found I was getting sleepy, so I prayed that the bull-fights would be good, and that it would be a fine fiesta, and that we would get some fishing. I wondered if there was anything else I might pray for, and I thought I would like to have some money, and then I started to think how I would make it, and thinking of money reminded me of the count, and I started wondering about where he was, and regretting I hadn't seen him since that night in Montmartre, and about something funny Brett told me about him, and as all the time I was kneeling with my forehead on the wood in front of me, and was thinking of myself as praying, I was a little ashamed, I regretted that I was such a rotten Catholic, but realized there was nothing I could do about it, at least for a while, and maybe never, but that anyway it was a grand religion, and I only wished I felt religious and maybe I would the next time. . . .

The contrast with the picture of the medieval man at prayer is obvious. (One may wonder whether it was really much different then, but, even so, our times have changed at least in the amount of truth that will be admitted.)

On another occasion, Brett and Jake go into San Fermin's to pray for Romero, the young bullfighter to whom Brett is attracted. But they are not there long before Brett stiffens.

"Come on," she whispered throatily, "Let's get out of here. Makes me damned nervous."
Outside in the hot brightness of the street Brett looked up at the tree-tops in the wind. The praying had not been much of a success.
"Don't know why I get so nervy in church," Brett said. "I've got the wrong type of face."

For these people, religion in our time is almost one with drawing magic circles and dancing for rain. It has a certain mysterious appeal; yet it is almost savagery when it appears in sophisticated surroundings. The church was neither spiritually nor architecturally tailored to stand next to noisy bars and cheap hotels, and the frequenters of the latter feel out of place in the former.

In some Hemingway characters the suspicion lingers that there was something worthwhile about the religious, and old Santiago promises to say ten Our Fathers and ten Hail Marys and to make a pilgrimage to the Virgen de Cobre if he catches a good fish. Yet he says, "I am not religious."

In other places, the repudiation of a personal God is complete. Such is the case in "The Snows of Kilimanjaro" where Harry gives a simple, emphatic cause-and-effect explanation of his wound, which began as a mere thorn scratch when he and Helen were photographing a herd of waterbuck. "I don't see why that had to happen to your leg," says Helen. "What have we done to have that happen to us?" Harry answers, "I suppose what I did was to forget to put iodine on it when I first scratched it."

Even more pointed is the Caliban-like passage near the end of A Farewell to Arms about the colony of ants on a log which Frederick Henry had once thrown on a campfire. He remembers his supreme indifference to the fate of the little creatures

as the flames licked up around the log. The nearest he came
to being their messiah was to throw a cup of water on them.
Actually the water steamed them, and he only wanted the
cup empty in order to drink whiskey from it. The whole
passage is a rather fine outburst of indignation against the great
impersonal "they" that breaks and kills those who are very
good or very strong in the world. It is pagan and virile—the
telling opposite of Christian faith in Hemingway's world, where
his opinion of even a good priest is "five-against-one," or
spiritual masturbation and infertility,[7] and where all religions
are "a joke" on all the people who have them.[8]

But where does the Nietzschean *Gott ist tot* lead? For most
existentialists, at least, it leads to a new kind of moral anarchy,
to an ethical solipsism in which there is a general agreement
of emphasis on pagan values, with a restoration of the natural
acts to precedence over the supernatural. It leads, as Nietzsche
put it, to a world that is beyond good and evil, to a world
where, in the words of Smerdyakov, "if there's no everlasting
God, there's no such thing as virtue, and no need of it."[9] And
it leads to a consequent accentuation of aesthetic style in all
of living, of the importance of imparting good form to life this
side the grave, since there is no other. As Helmut Kuhn says,
the nontheistic existentialists "invite us to pitch our tents in
the desert and forget about promised lands."[10]

Simone de Beauvoir strikes this chord in *The Mandarins,*
where Anne Dubreuilh says, "I've never felt sorry about losing
God, for he had robbed me of the earth," and Camus sounds
it in *The Myth of Sisyphus,* where he says that the cancellation
of man's eternal freedom restores and magnifies his freedom
here and now. Consequently, what counts is "not the best
living but the most living."[11] Sisyphus is a symbol of this
attitude. Accused of levity toward the gods and of purloining
their secrets, he was put in the underworld to the task of
repeatedly rolling a great stone to the top of a mountain,
from whence it always tumbled back again. One day he was
granted Pluto's permission to return to earth to chastise his

unloving wife. He returned to earth, and enjoyed it so much
that he refused to go back to the underworld until Mercury
was sent to fetch him. In his scorn of the gods, his hatred
of death, and his passion for life, all of which earned him the
penalty of exerting his whole being toward accomplishing
nothing, he was the absurd hero par excellence.

Nietzsche's *Also Sprach Zarathustra* reaches its climax on a
similar note. When Zarathustra has finally assembled a little
band of Higher Men, he comes one day into their cave and
finds them singing a strange litany and dancing around an ass
that periodically replies Hee-Haw to the whole business.
Alarmed, Zarathustra quickly repeats a kind of catechism-in-
reverse, in which he reminds them that they must become as
little children to enter the kingdom of heaven. "But we desire
not the kingdom of heaven," they reply. "We are become
men—*and therefore we desire the kingdom of earth*." And in
keeping with the Christian order of service, the Ugliest Man
gives a pagan testimony: "For this day's sake, *I* am for the first
time content to have lived my life. And to witness even so
much is not sufficient for me. It is worth while to live upon
earth: one day, one feast with Zarathustra, hath taught me to
love the earth."

To love the earth! That is the consummate value for life
without God.

Even Alyosha, the saintly Karamazov, says to Ivan, "One
longs to love with one's inside, with one's stomach. . . . I think
everyone should love life above everything in the world." And
Father Zossima, half of earth and half divine, the finest monk
ever drawn in a book, advised from his deathbed, "Kiss the
earth and love it with an unceasing, consuming love."

"Love is love and fun is fun," says Cantwell when he and
the Gran Maestro reveal to Renata the "major secret" of their
fraternal order. "But it is always so quiet when the gold fish
die." These tautologies are more than gibberish and more than
Gertrude Stein conundrums: they point by implication to a
whole world-truth: they deny that love leads to anything

beyond love or fun beyond fun. Love does not lead to any supreme Idea as it did for Plato. This is the stern code of our time, and it says simply, Love the earth, for there is nothing beyond. There is a long nihilistic passage in *Green Hills of Africa* which ends with an image that recalls Eliot's picture of the Thames in our day—"and the palm fronds of our victories, the worn light bulbs of our discoveries and the empty condoms of our great loves float with no significance against one single, lasting thing—the stream." The victories, the discoveries, the great loves—nothing leads to anything beyond its own sphere and time. So what is left but to love the earth?

And probably more than the characters of any other fictive world, or of any real world, for that matter, Hemingway's characters truly love the earth. It is pure *joie de vivre* that accounts for the bullfighter's loving the horns of the muscular death before him, or for old Santiago's calling the great fish that tortures him a friend and a brother (cf. Melville's Ahab: "Thou damned whale!"), or for Frederick Henry's defiance of the great impersonal "they." They would never say with Job, "Though *he* slay me, yet will I trust him," but they could say, and they do say, in so many words, "Though *life* slay me, yet will I love it."

The emphasis on the here and now is doubtless responsible for the new views on morality in our time, which generally allow, or at least pardon, all those acts which are deemed natural. Modern psychology has led, in at least one sense, around Sinai and back to the concept of pagan innocence, or behaving according to natural impulse. "Paganism," said Nietzsche, "is that which says yea to all that is natural, it is innocence in being natural, 'naturalness'. Christianity is that which says no to all that is natural, it is a certain lack of dignity in being natural; hostility to Nature."[12]

As it was the war and the experience of death that revealed "simplicity" to Hemingway, so it was the war that reduced his morality from the complicated Pharisaism of the twentieth-century church to the existentialism of Nietzschean ethics. It was given to Hawthorne "to dramatize the human soul," says John Peale Bishop; and, in our time, it was given to Hemingway to write "the drama of its disappearance." "The war made the traditional morality inacceptable," says Mr. Bishop; "it did not annihilate it; it revealed its immediate inadequacy. So that at its end, the survivors were left to face, as they could, a world without values."[13]

When God is overthrown and the world is without values, then the rebel must set up his own laws and moral codes. As one critic of Sartre has said, "On a shattered and deserted stage, without script, director, prompter, or audience, the actor is free to improvise his own part."[14] Or as another put it, when the stars are quenched in heaven, we tie a lamp to the masthead and steer by that.[15]

The basic integer of the new morality is the individual. "Yea," said Nietzsche, "this *I*, with its contradiction and confusion, reporteth most truly of its being—this creating, willing, valuing *I* that is the measure and the value of things."[16] Sartre likewise insists that the being of the self *is* value: "Value in its original upsurge is not posited by the for-itself; it is consubstantial with it."[17] As Nicolai Hartmann emphasized in his famous work on ethics, anything which takes precedence over man in ethics, be it God himself, perverts it and makes it immoral—man must rely on himself alone.

Beauvoir, too, emphasizes that true morality is not an agglomeration of principles, but a movement in which each man produces an authentic morality for himself. The great moralists of the past have not been imitators, but creators. *To be moral is to discover fundamentally one's own being.*[18]

Perhaps the best attempt of recent years to state the position of humanistic ethics is Erich Fromm's *Man for Himself,* which declares that "The duty to be alive is the same as the duty to become oneself, to develop into the individual one potentially is," and that "*good in humanistic ethics is the affirmation of life, the unfolding of man's powers. Virtue is responsibility toward his own existence.*" So long as man acknowledges his ethical dependence on any power or entity outside himself, says Fromm, he will remain dissatisfied, frustrated, and restless. The only solution to his ethical problem is "to face the truth, to acknowledge his fundamental aloneness and solitude in a universe indifferent to his fate. . . . Man must accept the responsibility for himself and the fact that only by using his own powers can he give meaning to his life."[19]

This emphasis on the self as the center of value is characteristic also of the Christian existentialists. Kierkegaard assigns every man to himself for the study of the ethical, for the ethical "is concerned with particular human beings, and with each and every one of them by himself," and "the ethical reality of the individual is the only reality."[20] Unamuno warns against founding an ethics on any dogma, for there is no dogma in the world that may not be moved; he prefers, like Beauvoir, "the ethics of ambiguity": "what I wish to establish is that uncertainty, doubt, perpetual wrestling with the mystery of our final destiny, mental despair, and the lack of any solid and stable dogmatic foundation, may be the basis of an ethic." His only principle of morality is this reworked passage from Letter XC of Sénancour's *Obermann:* "Man is perishable. That may be; but let us perish resisting, and if it is nothingness that awaits us, let us so act that it shall be an unjust fate."[21]

But this moral anarchy in which every man invents his own values is not the reign of irresponsibility nor the green signal of the Thélèmites' *Fais ce que voudras.* Actually, it becomes a most strenuous kind of ethics, in which every man's law is tailored to his private self, without even the laxity allowed for fitting in a pre-cut code imposed externally. Every man must make his own decision, *sans justification* and *sans excuse.*[22] Thus the full responsibility of his very existence rests on him and him alone.[23]

That is why Sartre, in *Huis Clos,* implies that hell is man-made. The hellishness is in the facticity to which man relegates himself when he either refuses to create his own values or creates the wrong ones. And that is close to the meaning of what Hemingway has to say about morals in *Death in the Afternoon*: "So far, about morals, I know only that what is moral is what you feel good after and what is immoral is what you feel bad after." If a man is moral in the absence of an artificial, superimposed morality, he feels good; but if he is immoral, he is giving himself hell. So Brett Ashley, after she decided not to be "one of those bitches that ruins children," told Jake Barnes, "I feel rather good you know. I feel rather set up."

Because the existentialist breaks the conventional moral pattern, he stands generally condemned by the traditional moralist, who cannot or will not understand how an individual ethics is really higher than a common ethics. The popular view of Hemingway's people is likely to be that with which Bill Grundy taunts Jake Barnes in *The Sun Also Rises*:

"You're an expatriate. You've lost touch with the soil. You get precious. Fake European standards have ruined you. You drink yourself to death. You become obsessed by sex. You spend all your time talking, not working. You are an expatriate, see? You hang around cafes."

Were Bill not an adroit ironist, I should wonder about Hemingway's intentions with regard to his surname. This is a Grundian viewpoint, all right, shared even by so eminent a critic as Clifton Fadiman.[24] But the Grundys fail to see the serious ethical and ontological foundation beneath the bizarre trappings of what may appear to be drunken pimpism and whorism. There are doubtless "fake European standards" as there are counterfeits of all concepts, but more candid observers might learn what James's Strether learned about them in *The Ambassadors,* that they are often the products of American misinterpretations of the real standards. As Robert Penn Warren has said, Jake and Brett dissipate "with a philosophical significance."[25]

But reproach is a price the innovator must pay; the world has always crucified individualists. They are strangers or outsiders, in the term of Camus, whose Meursault in *L'Étranger* is supposedly executed for a murder, but actually was himself murdered in the name of justice because he was not like the average man. Like Kafka's Joseph K., they are a minority in a world where the majority has other standards. Professor Stern, who taught at the Sorbonne, where Sartre's Mathieu Delarue is a teacher, displays a typical attitude when he glibly calls *Le Sursis* pornography and declares that as Retif de la Bretonne was called "the Rousseau of the gutter" Delarue should be styled "the Kierkegaard of the gutter."[26]

Those, however, who understand the genuine nature of the existential method realize the importance of its contribution to ethical thought. With its intense sincerity and personal applicability, it has fairly galvanized speculative morality in our day. As one writer has said, "M. Sartre is as uncompromising a moralist as Savonarola, and it is amusing to hear him spoken of as 'decadent' by persons who require no other proof than that the characters of his plays are so frequently psychopaths and murderers."[27] Uncompromising, yes. The existentialists are more severe in their self-governance than the Pharisees of Judaism—for they have no mercy on themselves. The maxim "Everything is permitted" does not lead to unreined libertinism in their ethics any more than it does in the ethics of Ivan Karamazov. When Henri says in Sartre's *Morts sans sépulture,* "To hell with the others. I owe an accounting only to myself now," he is consigning his actions to the sternest tribunal possible—to his own unyielding conscience.

Hemingway's heroes are likewise extremely rigorous with themselves. His background characters, the ethical bourgeoisie, are not. Each man categorizes himself as a hero or as one of the bourgeoisie according to the quality of his decisions. Life, like Hemingway's beloved bullfighting (which is in a sense a miniature theatre of life), is an art "in which the artist is in danger of death and in which the degree of brilliance in the performance is left to the fighter's honor." In Hemingway's Spain it is called *pundonor,* which means

honor, probity, courage, self-respect and pride in one word. Pride
is the strongest characteristic of the race and it is a matter of
pundonor not to show cowardice. . . . A bullfighter is not always
expected to be good, only to do his best. He is excused for bad
work if the bull is very difficult, he is expected to have off-days,
but he is expected to do the best he can with the given bull.[28]

The main idea in *pundonor* is that the individual chooses the
degree of severity and integrity by which he shall live, whether
he shall truly work close to the horns or try to fake a proximity
to them.

Jake Barnes and Robert Cohn in *The Sun Also Rises* make a
convenient illustration in contrast between the hero and the
cobarde. Jake lives in the typical existential tension, responsible to himself for all his actions; Robert, on the other hand,
behaves poorly and feels responsible for his behavior to all
those around him. When he knocks Jake out he comes to his
hotel room and begs his pardon. After brutally beating
Romero, he cries and wants to shake hands with him. But
the bullfighter displays better form in his determination to get
on his feet again and fight back.

The Hemingway initiate is tough; but, first of all, before he
is tough with anybody else, he is tough with himself. Albert
Tracy says of Harry Morgan, "Since he was a boy he never
had no pity for nobody. But he never had no pity for himself
either." Robert Jordan constantly checks his action and thinking to certify their correctness. For instance, after the incident
in which he shoots the Fascist cavalryman who rides upon him
and Maria in the sleeping-bag, he says to himself, "But you
behaved O.K. So far you have behaved all right." But it is
only *so far*—the tension will continue as long as he lives.

Since the author seems to be writing out the story of his own
life, it would naturally be expected that he be rigorous with
himself. And sure enough, in *Green Hills of Africa*, he avers
that "Every damned thing is your own fault if you're any
good." His relation to Cantwell is obvious, and Cantwell

blames himself even for forgetting to turn off an electric light
and for wasting an hour's electricity—"He regretted this as he
regretted all his errors."

Shortly before he leaves Venice, Cantwell buys Renata a
little ebony negro and has it sent to the hotel with a request
for Cipriani to pay for it and to expect repayment from him.
When the Colonel and Renata return to the hotel, Cipriani is
out. Renata says, "We haven't asked for the little negro that
will look after me."

"No," says the Colonel. "Because I did not want to ask for
him until Cipriani came in and I could pay him."

"Is everything that rigid?"

"With me, I guess," the Colonel says. "I'm sorry, daughter."

What Cantwell fears is that he will die without having paid
his debt. It reminds one of the dying hour of one of the earliest
existentialists on record, who said, "Pay Aesculapius the cock
that I owe him."

A case might be made for *pundonor's* being the point where
aesthetics invades ethics. It is entirely possible that true
ex-sistence may be viewed binocularly through aesthetics and
ethics and present a focused image, since it is really very
difficult to distinguish between them from an existential point
of view. As Kierkegaard put it, "Existing is an art. The
subjective thinker is aesthetic enough to give his life aesthetic
content, ethical enough to regulate it, and dialectical enough
to interpenetrate it with thought."[29] The new morality without
eternity, which is probably closer to that of the Greeks than
to anything since them, naturally aims at the full life; the love
of the earth leads to a definite emphasis on the aesthetic as
part of its this-world ethics.

Thomas Cash, whose work on Hemingway's relation to
death I have already mentioned, says that the interest in death
both stimulates the aesthetic interest and is part of it:

Only in contrast to death does life have meaning and, conversely,
death has meaning only when contrasted to life. A life must be

completely lived up to and including death before either has
meaning. And so the characters Hemingway creates drink everything, see everything, feel everything, do everything. Life to them
is a chain of varied links, each different, each exciting and uniquely
interesting, and the last link is the largest and most interesting of
all, the link of death.[30]

I believe Mr. Cash is mainly correct. I have suggested that
death is the traumatic experience that opens to Hemingway's
characters two ways of life, which for convenience I denomi-
nated the "simple" and the "complicated." Now all of those
who maintain a simple existence in Hemingway's fiction are
also the same ones who strive to give aesthetic content to their
lives. I believe this is because their ethics of existence, and
the very questions of living and dying, are aesthetic in nature:
to *ex-sist*, to stand out from all other being, is automatically to
assume an aesthetic factor.

For Hemingway, there is very definitely a correct way to
live and a correct way to die, and his heroes are heroes because
they choose the way that imparts form to their lives. The
awareness of form begins early in the Nick Adams stories. The
young Nick of "Indian Camp" is already sensitive to his surroundings. The advance of his sensitivity between these early
years and his young maturity is apparent in "Cross-Country
Snow," where he exults in Alpine skiing. And skiing is also a
topic of conversation in "An Alpine Idyll," where Nick and
John are glad to get down from the mountains because they
have stayed too long and the spring sun has made the snow
too bright:

I was glad to be down away from snow. It was too late in the
spring to be up in the Silvretta. I was a little tired of skiing. We
had stayed too long. I could taste the snow water we had been
drinking melted off the tin roof of the hut. The taste was a part
of the way I felt about skiing. I was glad there were other things
beside skiing, and I was glad to be down, away from the unnatural
high mountain spring, into this May morning in the valley.

A little later Nick says, "I'd forgotten what beer tasted like."

"I hadn't," John said. "Up in the hut I used to think about it a lot."
"Well," I said, "we've got it now."
"You oughtn't to ever do anything too long."
"No. We were up there too long."
"Too damn long," John said. "It's no good doing a thing too long."

The same idea is expressed by Harry in "The Snows of Kilimanjaro" when he gets bored with the slowness of his death:

"It's a bore," he said out loud.
"What is, my dear?"
"Anything you do too bloody long."

Doing anything "too bloody long" vitiates the aesthetic enjoyment it offers.

Since Hemingway is a proud outdoorsman, it is natural that his joy in the correct form is often connected with various kinds of sport. One of the finest pieces of prose he has done is the Thoreauvian "Big Two-Hearted River." In this story, the reader gets all the majesty of North American scenery as seen through Nick's eyes as he hikes along the road in search of the right place to fish, he thrills with Nick at the right way to camp, and he feels his mouth beginning to water as Nick discusses the right way to cook on a campfire. In Part Two of the story, Nick demonstrates the right way to fish. Once he leaves the fishing for a few minutes and crawls up on the bank to light a cigarette because "he did not want to rush his sensations any." And in "Now I Lay Me," a later story, he lies on an army cot on the other side of the world and remembers the various ways in which his fishing back home constituted an aesthetic experience. As the point is made in "Banal Story," "there is romance everywhere" if form is imparted everywhere.

Pilar, in *For Whom the Bell Tolls*, even remembers the

exquisite form of her love-making in Valencia when she was young. Her recollections are an almost Keatsian catalogue of sensuousness:

"We ate in pavilions on the sand. Pastries made of cooked and shredded fish and red and green peppers and small nuts like grains of rice. Pastries delicate and flaky and the fish of a richness that was incredible. Prawns fresh from the sea sprinkled with lime juice. They were pink and sweet and there were four bites to a prawn. Of those we ate many. Then we ate *paella* with fresh sea food, clams in their shells, mussels, crayfish, and small eels. Then we ate even smaller eels alone cooked in oil and as tiny as bean sprouts and curled in all directions and so tender they disappeared in the mouth without chewing. All the time drinking a white wine, cold, light and good at thirty centimos the bottle. And for an end, melon. That is the home of the melon."

"The melon of Castile is better," Fernando said.

"*Que va,*" said the woman of Pablo. "The melon of Castile is for self abuse. The melon of Valencia for eating. When I think of those melons long as one's arm, green like the sea and crisp and juicy to cut and sweeter than the early morning in summer. Aye, when I think of those smallest eels, tiny, delicate and in mounds on the plate. Also the beer in pitchers all through the afternoon, the beer sweating in its coldness in pitchers the size of water jugs."

"And what did thee when not eating nor drinking?"

"We made love in the room with the strip wood blinds hanging over the balcony and a breeze through the opening of the top of the door which turned on hinges. We made love there, the room dark in the day time from the hanging blinds, and from the streets there was the scent of the flower market and the smell of burned powder from the firecrackers of the *traca* that ran through the streets exploding each noon during the Feria. . . ."

Colonel Cantwell in *Across the River and into the Trees* has similar interests, as a gourmand as well as a lover. When he and Renata eat lobster at the Gritti, he explains to her that it is the best of lobsters, because it has filled with the moon. He says a lobster that has filled in the dark is not worth eating.

Later, as he walks through the Venetian market, he notes in some sausage he tastes "the half-smokey, black peppercorned, true flavor of the meat from hogs that ate acorns in the mountains." To him, the market is "the closest thing to a good museum like the Prado or as the Accademia is now." Real art is not all enclosed in buildings with marble pillars.

All of the sensuous thrills are not gustatory and sexual, however; in the same novel in which Pilar appears Hemingway writes of Sordo dying on a hilltop:

Dying was nothing and he had no picture of it nor fear of it in his mind. But living was a field of grain blowing in the wind on the side of a hill. Living was a hawk in the sky. Living was an earthen jar of water in the dust of the threshing with the grain flailed out and the chaff blowing. Living was a horse between your legs and a carbine under one leg and a hill and valley and a stream with trees along it and the far side of the valley and the hills beyond.

Life is equated with sensations, because existence is equated with form.

In *To Have and Have Not* Hemingway gets back to the proper way to fish. Harry Morgan is disgusted with his employer's "messy" approach to deep-sea fishing:

Johnson took the harness off the reel so he could put the rod across his knees because his arms got tired holding it in position all the time. Because his hands got tired holding the spool of the reel against the drag of the big bait, he screwed the drag down when I wasn't looking. I never knew he had it down. I didn't like to see him hold the rod that way but I hated to be crabbing at him all the time. Besides, with the drag off, line would go out so there wasn't any danger. But it was a sloppy way to fish.

A huge black marlin hits the line and the butt of the rod socks Johnson in the stomach and the whole rig is lost overboard. Johnson is bewildered.

"What would I do if I was hooked to a fish like that?" Johnson said.

"That's what you wanted to fight all by yourself," I told him.

"They're too big," Johnson said, "Why, it would just be punishment."

"Listen," I said. "A fish like that would kill you. . . ."

"Well," said Johnson, "they're too big. If it isn't enjoyable, why do it?"

"That's right, Mr. Johnson," Eddy said. "If it isn't enjoyable, why do it? Listen, Mr. Johnson. You hit the nail on the head there. If it isn't enjoyable—why do it?"

Johnson, of course, is the typical, crass, middle-class American. He fishes only because the travel folders say that everybody does it. He is unauthentic, and likewise unaesthetic.

Green Hills of Africa is almost a diary of form. Early in the first chapter the stage is set for an excursion into the realm of the hypersensory, as Hemingway rides along the sandy track of road, looking at the thick brush that passes in the dark, feeling the cool wind of the night, smelling "the good smell of Africa," and feeling altogether happy. He is going to hunt, and hunt properly.

The way to hunt is for as long as you live against as long as there is such and such an animal; just as the way to paint is as long as there is you and colors and canvas, and to write as long as you can live and there is pencil and paper or ink or any machine to do it with. . . .

Kandisky cannot understand why Hemingway wants to kill a kudu. "What is killing a kudu, anyway?" he asks. "You should not take it so seriously. It is nothing. In a year you kill twenty." But Hemingway wants to kill them according to a certain form—he wants one at the salt lick. As Pop says, "The trouble is you're working on them where they are smart. They've been shot at there ever since there's been salt." "That's what makes it fun," answers Hemingway. He is like

Droopy, the tracker whom he admired because he was "a great stylist in everything he did." With no God and no religion in our time, ritual—giving form to the mysterious—passes from the church to the great outdoors and the whole of secular life.

Throughout the entire expedition, Hemingway tries to get a bigger bull than Karl. Karl is a poor shot, a messy hunter, unable to climb, unsporting, but extremely lucky. Finally, when the Wanderobo-Masai takes Hemingway to the unhunted little pocket that seems like a hunter's Garden of Eden, he kills a massive bull with a 52-inch horn span. He returns in elation to the rest of the party and finds that Karl has stumbled onto three unbelievably large kudu, and has shot one with a 57-inch horn span. "They were the biggest, widest, darkest, longest-curling, heaviest, most unbelievable pair of kudu horns in the world." But Pop gives the key when he consoles Hemingway: "You can always remember how you shot them. That's what you really get out of it." The form's the thing.

Since violence and death are such an integral part of his world, Hemingway is understandably much concerned about the form his characters assume under the pressure of suffering and dying. As a frightened young ambulance driver in Italy, he received the perennial talisman from Shakespeare: "By my troth, I care not: a man can die but once; we owe God a death . . . and let it go which way it will, he that dies this year is quit for the next." Wilson quotes it to Macomber in "The Short Happy Life," Cantwell rephrases it in *Across the River and into the Trees*,[31] and Hemingway passes it on to the military of the second World War in the introduction to his collection of war stories called *Men at War*. Casual bravery had early become part of the Hemingway code and part of the artistic approach to death.

His priests (who have abandoned freedom and responsibility in religion) and politicians (whose real existence is lost in deference to public opinion) generally die badly, with "very little dignity."[32] His individualistic heroes, on the other hand, live by the motto of Cantwell: "Better to die on our feet than to live on our knees." The phrase is used (without acknowl-edgment to Hemingway) in Camus' *Rebel* as a proper slogan for the man in revolt.[33] The bartender has another motto, which he repeats to Cantwell: "Better to live one day as a lion than a hundred years as a sheep."

Hemingway the veteran hunter has great respect for the lion as an animal that meets death with dignity. In "The Short Happy Life of Francis Macomber," after the lion has been wounded and has gone into the brush, Hemingway writes: "All of him, pain, sickness, hatred and all of his remaining strength, was tightening into an absolute concentration for a rush." A good bull will likewise behave with dignity, changing in the same part of the ring time and again with the steel in him, paying no attention to the punishment he receives. As another aficionado has said of life and bullfights, "Every battle with death is lost before it begins. The splendour of the battle cannot lie in its outcome, but only in the dignity of the act."[34]

But the death of the hyena is completely another thing, bereft of all dignity and belonging to the comical:

Highly humorous was the hyena obscenely loping, full belly dragging, at daylight on the plain, who, shot from the stern, skittered on into speed to tumble end over end. Mirth provoking was the hyena that stopped out of range by an alkali lake to look back, and, hit in the chest, went over on his back, his four feet and his full belly in the air. Nothing could be more jolly than the hyena coming suddenly wedge-headed and stinking out of high grass by a *donga*, hit at ten yards, who raced his tail in three narrowing, scampering circles until he died. It was funny to M'Cola to see a hyena shot at close range. There was that comic slap of the bullet and the hyena's agitated surprise to find death inside of him. It was funnier to see a hyena shot at a great distance, in the heat shimmer of the plain, to see him go over backwards, to see him start that frantic circle, to see that electric speed that meant that he was racing the little nickelled death inside him. But the great joke of all, the thing M'Cola waved his hands across his face about, and turned away and shook his head and laughed, ashamed even of the hyena; the pinnacle of hyenic humor, was the hyena, the classic hyena, that hit too far back while running, would circle madly, snapping and tearing at himself until he pulled his own intestines out, and then stood there, jerking them out and eating them with relish.[35]

The dialectic of the brave and the cowardly is between the lion and the hyena, and Hemingway respects only his men who suffer and die in a leonine manner.

Suicide is cowardice, and belongs to the hyenic acts, eating one's own intestines with relish. It is mutely condemned in the Indian of the slit throat in "Indian Camp." As Camus says, suicide is the big question:\ "Judging whether life is or is not worth living amounts to answering the fundamental question of philosophy."[36] And Hemingway feels ashamed for men who answer it negatively. Perhaps it is in expiation for his own father's suicide, to which he doubtless alludes in *For Whom the Bell Tolls*, where Jordan remembers with shame how the gun was handed to him—the gun with which his father had murdered himself—and how he took it up to the lake above Red Lodge and threw it down into eight hundred feet of water.

Then, as he thought, he realized that if there was any such thing as ever meeting, both he and his grandfather would be acutely embarrassed by the presence of his father. Any one has a right to do it, he thought. But it isn't a good thing to do. I understand it, but I do not approve of it. *Lache* was the word. But you *do* understand it? Sure I understand it but. Yes, but. You have to be awfully occupied with yourself to do a thing like that.

"I'll never forget," Jordan thinks, "how sick it made me the first time I knew he was a *cobarde*. Go on, say it in English. Coward."

The lion-hyena contrast is clearly defined between Harry Morgan and the Negro Wesley when they are both wounded while carrying contraband liquor. Harry's wound is by far the more serious, and does lead to the amputation of a limb. Yet he is the quiet one, while Wesley, with a superficial wound, moans continuously about being shot and dying. When Harry is finally shot fatally, alone on his boat and unable to steer, with a burning thirst, he cuts the lines to the motor to prevent fire and crawls to the cockpit. His only complaint is a remonstrance of himself for failing to kill the Cuban thoroughly. "He lay on his back and tried to breathe steadily. . . . At first he tried to brace himself against the roll with his good hand. Then he lay quietly and took it."

"Taking it" is all-important to dignity. Cayetano Ruiz, the cardplayer in "The Gambler, the Nun, and the Radio," stoically bears the pain of two bullets in the abdomen and, finally, the paralysis of a leg. His silent behavior is the opposite of that of the Russian beet-worker who was accidentally wounded in the thigh and who screams constantly in the hospital. Ruiz will not even tell the police-detective who shot him. "Listen," the detective says, "this isn't Chicago. You're not a gangster. You don't have to act like a moving picture." But, as Young observes, he *does* have to act like a moving picture—it is part of the code of grace under pressure that belongs to all of Hemingway's heroes.[37]

It belongs to Frederick Henry, of whom Rinaldi says when he comes to the hospital after Henry has been severely wounded, "You are so brave and quiet I forget you are suffering."

It belongs to Manuel Garcia, a bullfighter known professionally as Maera, whom Hemingway openly admires in *Death in the Afternoon*. All the last year he fought he knew he was going to die:

He had galloping consumption and he expected to die before the year was out. In the meantime he was very occupied. He was gored badly twice but he paid no attention to it. I saw him fight on a Sunday with a five-inch wound in his armpit that he received on a Thursday. I saw the wound, saw it dressed before and after the fight and he paid no attention to it. It hurt as a torn wound made by a splintered horn hurts after two days but he paid no attention to the pain. He acted as though it were not there. He did not favor it or avoid lifting the arm; he ignored it. He was a long way beyond pain. I never saw a man to whom time seemed so short as it did to him that season.

The next time I saw him he had been gored in the neck in Barcelona. The wound was closed with eight stitches and he was fighting, his neck bandaged, the day after. His neck was stiff and he was furious. He was furious at the stiffness he could do nothing about and the fact that he had to wear a bandage that showed above his collar.

Once, during a fight, his sword struck a vertebra and his wrist broke. With the broken wrist, he made five more attempts to kill the bull, succeeding on the fifth. He need not have done it the hard way:

Now at any time he could have, without danger or pain, slipped the sword into the neck of the bull, let it go into the lung or cut the jugular and killed him with no trouble. But his honor demanded that he kill him high up between the shoulders, going in as a man should, over the horn, following the sword with his body.

It is still the code of *pundonor*, a mysterious mixture of pride, dignity, defiance, and honor. It is a code for those who face death often and are not afraid.

It is this quiet, manly behavior that earns the highest respect of which Hemingway is capable for the man who died on the cross. Five times in the brief scenario "Today is Friday," the first soldier says of Jesus, "He was pretty good in there today." He refers, of course, to the noble manner in which Christ bore suffering and death. This little story, with its anachronous bar scene, is a vivid statement of Hemingway's opinion of our situation today: all the soldiers can do is order another brandy and praise the *human* side of God.

The old man of the sea, who "took his suffering as it came," is almost a classical symbol of the dignity of humanism. "I will show them," he says, "what a man can do and what a man

endures." After the great fish has jerked him forward into the
floor of the boat, with his face in the butchered dolphin and
the line racing singeingly through his hand, he puts the hand
into the salt water and draws it out. "It is not bad," he says.
"And pain does not matter to a man."

When the galanos had devoured the body of his fish and the
old man had spit up blood with the feeling that something
had broken inside him, "He knew he was beaten now finally
and without remedy." But unlike the old man of the *Esquire*
article who was the real-life model for the story,[38] he does not
cry and become hysterical. He has been beaten by going out
too far, but he will go out again.

There is obvious Christological imagery in *The Old Man and
the Sea*. Like the Christ of the passion, Santiago goes out
alone, without even the boy (John, in Jesus' case). As Christ
was three days and nights in the tomb, Santiago is three days
and nights on the water—and both the tomb and the water are
womb symbols. As Christ fell beneath the cross, Santiago
falls beneath his mast. As the heart of Christ broke, so that
water flowed mingled with blood from the wound in his side,
the old man feels something break inside of him. Both have
marred hands—Christ from the nails, and Santiago from the
fishing line. "Ay," ejaculates Santiago as the line runs through
his hand—a cry such as might escape from a man's lips when
nails go through his hands. All of these parallels, and the
constant references of Christ in the New Testament to fishing,
even the ichthyological symbol which came to be the sign of
New Testament Christianity—all of these argue that Santiago
may be a kind of Christ. But, if he is, it is the Christ who "was
good in there today," the humanistic Christ in a world without
God, not the metaphysical Christ.

All gods are dead, and man is thrown back upon himself
with the responsibility of forging his self out of a private
ethics and a private aesthetic. Paradoxically, the only peace in
our time is the strenuous no-peace, the continuous striving to
mold life, moment-by-moment, from a dreadful nothingness
into an ethically and aesthetically authentic form.

CHAPTER FIVE

THE ONE AND THE MANY

IT IS A generally held assumption that the thought of Ernest Hemingway, as he grew older and as the world became more political in the nineteen-thirties, underwent a definite socialization. Maxwell Geismar's representative article, "No Man Alone Now,"[1] had as its thesis the idea that with Harry Morgan's dying words, "A man ain't got no bloody f——g chance alone," Hemingway was announcing his return to society, and was oscillating from the "separate peace" of Nick Adams and Lt. Henry to the "no man is an island" theme of *The Fifth Column* and *For Whom the Bell Tolls*.

But the pendulum, having in the 'thirties swung toward socialization, in the early 'fifties swung back again to individualism with *Across the River and into the Trees* (harsh old Cantwell may very well be the same soldier who in the earlier World War made a separate peace) and *The Old Man and the Sea*. Though Hemingway was influenced by the political pressures of the late 'twenties and the 'thirties, through it all he held true to his original world view, not so much deviating from his position as expanding it.

The "no man is an island" theme is not incompatible with the subjective emphasis of existentialism. All of the major existentialists in our century have faced up squarely to the problem of the one and the many, and there has been in their answers a decided unanimity in favor of the brotherhood of man.

It is true that existentialism is a philosophy of freedom—but freedom to act *within a situation,* not freedom to elude situation. Sartre's Mathieu Delarue pursues his freedom through two and a half volumes of *Les Chemins de la liberté.* He is so obsessed with the abstract idea of being free that he zealously guards himself against all entanglements—so zealously, in fact, that he even forsakes Marcelle and the baby she is to bear him lest he become involved. But, the fact is, he is never really free because he lingers in no situation where he might act with freedom; not until he joins the guerrilla movement and submits himself to the war of the group does he truly become an *ex-sisting* individual, acting freely in *l'engagement.*

Similarly, Orestes, in *Les Mouches,* does not really become Orestes until he undertakes the emancipation of Argos. So long as he plans to flee the city as an unknown, he remains Philebus; when he determines to slay Clytemnestra and Aegisthus, he becomes Orestes. Existence is in the act. As Benoit Pruche has said, Orestes' crime is the beginning of his liberty and of his existence.[2]

Camus' early novel, *The Stranger,* dealt exclusively with the theme of isolation. In *The Plague,* however, he dealt also with the involvement motif. Rambert, who wished to escape from the pestilential city of Oran, at the very brink of his freedom turned back and remained with the plague and its victims. His real character, his freedom, lay there. To desert, under the circumstances, would have been to forgo the arrival at true selfhood, which could be reached only in situation.

Jean-Baptiste Clamence, in Camus' last book *The Fall,* also considers escape, but of a different nature. The escape that beckons invitingly to him is suicide—"the right to disappear definitively." His involvement is the whole business of living, of being himself. But he has long retreated from his true being, and has, as he himself put it, played a role, that of the respectable judge with a sterling heart, an unimpeachable character, and philanthropic motives. He played the role well. Everyone thought he was sincere in it. Even *he* thought so, until a hideous laugh out of his subconscious began to crack his mask. Then he realized the truth: "I was absent at the moment when I took up the most space."

Clamence is now faced with a choice: suicide or honesty, self-murder or self-affirmation, escape or involvement. He chooses honest selfhood and involvement. He no longer hides the irrespectable side of his life from others: he tells indecent stories to those whom he considers most likely to be shocked; he spits in the faces of the blind; in short, he reveals a character almost the opposite of what he had once shown. And, moreover, the judge becomes a judge-penitent, confessing his lies to others, in order that they may be involved in his evangel of confession by recognizing in his sins their sins also. Death would perhaps have been easier—that, says Camus, a man must decide for himself as the first real philosophical question—but he chose the harder part in choosing involvement in his own situation. But not only his, for all men are involved in the Fall.

Hemingway probably has even less sympathy than Sartre and Camus for those who attempt to escape from their involvement. He is familiar with the various ways by which soldiers try to get out of battle. In *A Farewell to Arms*, Lt. Henry runs upon a soldier who threw away his truss "so it would get bad and I wouldn't have to go to the line again," and he asks Miss Van Campen, the stuffy hospital director, if she has ever known a man who tried to escape the war by kicking himself in the scrotum. Col. Cantwell catalogues other methods of malingering, such as self-inflicted calf wounds, the matchboxes of gonorrheal pus, and the ten-centime pieces put under armpits to produce jaundice.

Other Hemingway characters who try to remove themselves from their situations are the man in "Hills Like White Elephants," who, like Mathieu Delarue, wants his girl friend to have an abortion to obviate the engagement of fatherhood; the boy in "God Rest You Merry, Gentlemen," who castrates himself because of an erection phobia; and Pablo in *For Whom the Bell Tolls,* who deserts Jordan and his friends but is saved in the end by returning to situation. The removal constitutes a retreat from the true being of the self.

Cantwell expresses the real existentialist position with regard to engagement when he is thinking about the reasons why he cannot marry Renata and have five sons to send to the corners of the earth: "I guess the cards we draw are those we get. You wouldn't like to re-deal would you dealer? No. They only deal to you once, and then you pick them up and play them." It is as simple a matter as playing the cards that are dealt us. So when Harry Morgan says he has no choice but to ferry the Cubans, what he means is that he must play the cards as they have been dealt him. He does not really *have* to carry them.

I could stay right here, he thought, and there wouldn't be anything. I could stay right here and have a few drinks and get hot and I wouldn't be in it. . . . All I've got is my *cojones* to peddle. . . . I could just let it slide and do nothing.

But his cards say that all he has to peddle is his *cojones;* so he accepts the situation and reconstitutes the being that is known as Harry Morgan.

One of the situations dealt us in life is the contest for the freedom of all. But how is the extreme subjectivism of the existentialist reconciled to the discipline and objectivism of war and the mass-force?

Sartre says that the individual is responsible not only for his own individuality but for all men;[3] and Beauvoir asserts that every man needs the freedom of every other man, for only the freedom of others prevents us from hardening into facticity.[4] Karl Jaspers avows this as the whole thesis of his philosophizing: "The individual cannot become human by himself. Self-being is only real in communication with other self-being. Alone, I sink into gloomy isolation. . . . My own freedom can only exist if the other is also free."[5]

One author has juxtaposed quotations from Beauvoir and John Donne in a passage concerning this problem:

A man's most fundamental choice is of himself. And yet what one wants for oneself, one wants for everyone. If one is free, everyone must be. This is another way of explaining the sentence, "One cannot be free in a vacuum." Free men require free men; or, as Simone de Beauvoir has said, "I am flung into the world amid these alien liberties. . . . I have need of others." "No man is an island," although it is out of the feeling for oneself as an island that existentialism with its imperative for responsible action springs.[6]

Several existentialists have come remarkably close to stating the "no man is an island" theme as Donne stated it. Kierkegaard once wrote, "If an individual could fall away from the race entirely, his falling away would involve a modification of the race."[7] Unamuno, in the same book with his most eloquent passage on the majesty of the individual, has written, "But man does not live alone; he is not an isolated individual, but a member of society. There is not a little truth in the saying that the individual, like the atom, is an abstraction."[8] And Karl Jaspers, comparing modern existential thought to classical Greek humanism, said of the Greeks, "They lived in the freedom that requires every man to answer for his own life, jointly with all others. Community, according to a saying of those sages, means to feel a wrong that is done unto others as if it were done unto myself."[9]

So when Hemingway writes in *To Have and Have Not* that a man hasn't got a bloody chance alone, when in *The Fifth Column* he subjects Philip Rawlings to party discipline for the duration, and when in *For Whom the Bell Tolls* he begins by quoting Donne's "No man is an island, entire of itself. . . . therefore never send to know for whom the bell tolls, it tolls for thee," and then dramatizes it for our times through four-hundred-seventy-odd pages, he is no more being inconsistent with his earlier and later emphasis on individualism than the greatest exponents of existentialism. He is simply expanding his treatment of the individual as the individual is related to the whole of humanity, and at a time when a man must not, as Anselmo accuses Pablo of doing, put "thy fox-hole before the interests of humanity."

Doubtless, Hemingway, like the French existentialists, was moved to the social treatment of his work by the fermentation of world conditions at the time, and Jordan speaks of "the cause" for the same reasons as Sartre's dedicated ones in *Les Mains sales*. Jordan even feels a brotherhood with others in the cause. Recalling his days at Gaylord's and at the Fifth Regiment Headquarters, he thinks:

> At either of those places you felt that you were taking part in a crusade. That was the only word for it although it was a word that had been so worn and abused that it no longer gave its true meaning. You felt, in spite of all bureaucracy and inefficiency and party strife something that was like the feeling you expected to have and did not have when you made your first communion. It was a feeling of consecration to a duty toward all of the oppressed of the world which would be as difficult and embarrassing to speak about as religious experience and yet it was authentic as the feeling you had when you heard Bach, or stood in Chartres Cathedral or the Cathedral at Leon and saw the light coming through the great windows; or when you saw Mantegna and Greco and Brueghel in the Prado. It gave you a part in something that you could believe in wholly and completely and in which you felt an absolute brotherhood with the others who were engaged in it. It was something that you had never known before but that you had experienced now and you gave such importance to it and the reasons for it that your own death seemed of complete unimportance; only a thing to be avoided because it would interfere with the performance of your duty.

There is much talk in this novel about duty and discipline, words that Hemingway would ordinarily eschew. Yet they are necessary in time of war. As Beauvoir points out in *The Ethics of Ambiguity*, wars are won by brute force, and men must supply that force by voluntarily suspending their subjective, individual natures for the interim. "Since we can conquer our enemies only by acting upon their facticity, by reducing them to things, we have to make ourselves things." The first and basic sacrifice of a soldier is of his own freedom of thought and action.[10]

So Rawlings and Jordan, still Hemingway heroes, become ciphers in the struggle for the freedom of all. Jordan intrinsically resents Golz's orders for what they will do to him and to Maria and the others. Yet

that is not the way to think, he told himself, and there is not you, and there are no people that things must not happen to. Neither you nor this old man is anything. You are instruments to do your duty. There are necessary orders that are no fault of yours and there is a bridge and that bridge can be the point on which the future of the human race can turn.

Even though they seem impossible of success, orders should be carried out.

The situation is very much like that of the French Resistance forces during the Occupation, as described by Sartre in "The Republic of Silence."[11] Members of the Underground acted with total responsibility on orders that came from men or women whom they did not even know. There was equality of risk for the private and the commander-in-chief. Duty consumed individuality.

But, as Beauvoir says, subsequent to the statement that men must become objects in time of war, as soon as war is over, the individual takes up his freedom again. An illustration of the fact on a large scale is the principle of the war trial—legally trying a few war criminals for the thousands of murders and atrocities for which they were responsible rather than peremptorily executing them—the principle that the dignity of individual human right must be reestablished as that for which the war was waged.[12] Therefore when Henri, in Beauvoir's novel *The Mandarins,* considers that the war is over, he thinks: "Four years of austerity, four years of working only for others —that was a lot, that was too much. It was time now for him to think a little about himself."

Hemingway's Jordan dreams often of a day when the war will be over for him, and he can resume his freedom and he and Marie can go to Gaylord's together and sleep in a hotel together and he can buy some books in Madrid and send Luis the porter out for a bottle of absinthe. And Hemingway himself, when the war was over and the people of the world were busy resuming the lives they had laid aside years ago, began to concentrate once more on his hero as an individual, and wrote that quiet classic of individualism, *The Old Man and the Sea.*

As Sartre says, war is *my* war as if *I* chose it, and I bear the responsibility of it[13]—but nothing can make me like it. The existentialist subscribes to the doctrine of the brotherhood of all men, especially in a time when the freedom of all men is at stake. But at the earliest moment possible he heads cross-country to the "separate peace."

CHAPTER SIX

THE HERO IN LOVE

"WHAT DO YOU value most?" asks Count Greffi of Lt. Henry in *A Farewell to Arms*.

"Someone I love."

"With me it is the same. That is not wisdom."

This is the anomaly of Hemingway's position on women. The way of the whorehouse is preferable to legitimate love because it does not lead to complications; yet Hemingway's heroes are paragons of virility, and, as such, demand the companionship of real women. Where is the neutral ground between *Men Without Women* (which Professor Baker says was a twist of Ford Madox Ford's *Men and Women*) and the amatory idealism of *For Whom the Bell Tolls?* How are love and the fear of complications to be reconciled?

The simplest solution is found in the fact that Hemingway divides his women into the good and the bad, according to the extent to which they complicate a man's life. Those who are simple, who participate in relationships with the heroes and yet leave the heroes as free as possible, receive sympathetic treatment; those who are demanding, who constrict the liberty of the heroes, who attempt to possess them, are the women whom men can live without. Into the former category fall the little Indian girls of the Nick Adams stories, Harry Morgan's

wife, Catherine Henry, Maria, and Renata; into the latter, the
Marjorie of the Nick Adams tales, Mrs. Macomber, and Dorothy
of *The Fifth Column.*

On the man's side, Sartre defines love as an attempt to
absorb the Other, to make the Other dependent on and
amenable to oneself, or to enslave the Other in order to be free
oneself. Love is the wish to be loved, to become all in all to the
Other and thus assimilate his freedom into mine.[1]

Pruche's definition is sacrificial, or that of the Other:

> Aimer, c'est donc *me* mettre *librement* à la disposition d'autrui
> pour qu'il puisse, en m'utilisant, répondre à *sa* vocation personelle
> d'existant, dans le sens du mode de réalisation librement choisi de
> *son* libre projet fondamental, c'est-à-dire dans la ligne des réalisa-
> tions concrètes de son "drôle de petit sens" de structure existentielle.[2]

To love is to put myself freely at the disposition of the other
person. In a man's world like Hemingway's this would be the
more acceptable definition for *female* love. It is proper there
that the so-called weaker sex surrender its freedom to the
freedom of the male. Woman should have, in Gabriel Marcel's
terminology, *disponibilité*—she should be "available" to the
male and capable of losing *her* self in the being of *his* self.

Simone de Beauvoir, who has written very brilliantly from
a female viewpoint on the subject of the psychology of sex,
agrees that it is very much a man's world, and, though she says
it in other words, implies that men love by Sartre's definition
and women by Pruche's:

> Men have found it possible to be passionate lovers at certain
> times in their lives, but there is not one of them who could be called
> "a great lover"; in their most violent transports, they never abdicate
> completely; even on their knees before a mistress, what they still
> want is to take possession of her; at the very heart of their lives
> they remain sovereign subjects; the beloved woman is only one
> value among others; they wish to integrate her into their existence
> and not to squander it entirely on her. For woman, on the contrary,
> to love is to relinquish everything for the benefit of a master.[3]

Or, in Byron's words, "Man's love is of man's life a thing apart; 'Tis woman's whole existence." The woman in love says of her man as the Baptist said of Jesus, "He must increase, I must decrease." True love, from a female viewpoint in a man's world, is an annihilation of self and the self's ambitions for the sake of the other.

There is a place for this kind of love in Hemingway's world.

Harry Morgan's wife is Mme. Beauvoir's dependent woman in love: when he dies she doesn't know what to do, or how she will get through the nights alone. She has never tried to possess him, but has completely given herself to him.

Catherine is so absorbed in Henry that she even wants to cut her hair to be like him. She says, "Why, darling, I don't live at all when I'm not with you. . . . I want you to have a life. I want you to have a fine life. But we'll have it together, won't we?" In Hemingway's opinion this is surely the ideal love of a woman for a man—a love in which she loses her being but has it in the being of her man.

If Col. Cantwell is Ernest Hemingway, then Cantwell's girl Renata is surely what Hemingway wants his woman to be, an intelligent creature who nevertheless in her love makes herself a pawn for her man. She allows him to direct their lives together—he orders her food, recommends her drinks, appoints her meetings, and times their love-makings. Perhaps such a one is truly more of a "daughter" than a mate.

But Hemingway's supreme expression of love is, and is likely to remain, that of Jordan and Maria in *For Whom the Bell Tolls*. It most strongly expresses the desire of the lovers for a mystical union in which the two lovers become one. The idea was present in the Catherine-Henry relationship (Catherine said, "We really are the same one"), but here it is treated extensively.

It begins in the sleeping-bag, when Maria says,

"We will be as one animal in the forest and be so close that neither one can tell that one of us is one and not the other. Can you not feel my heart be your heart?"

"Yes. There is no difference."

"Now, feel. I am thee and thou art me and all of one is the other. And I love thee, oh, I love thee so. Are we not truly one? Canst thou not feel it?"

"Yes," he said. "It is true."

"And feel now. Thou hast no heart but mine."

"Nor any other legs, nor feet, nor of the body."

Again she says, "But we will be one now and there will never be a separate one. . . . I will be thee when thou are not there." And later, when she is holding the horses and worrying about Robert at the bridge, she decides to pray for him "because I am not here. There isn't any me. I am only with him."

"The supreme goal of human love, as of mystical love," says Beauvoir,

is identification with the loved one. The measure of values, the truth of the world, are in his consciousness; hence it is not enough to serve him. The woman in love tries to see with his eyes; she reads the book he reads, prefers the pictures and the music he prefers; she is interested only in the landscapes she sees with him, in the ideas that come from him; she adopts his friendships, his enmities, his opinions; and when she questions herself, it is his reply she tries to hear; she wants to have in her lungs the air he has already breathed; the fruits and flowers that do not come from his hands have no taste and no fragrance. Her idea of location in space, even, is upset: the center of the world is no longer the place where she is, but that occupied by her lover; all roads lead to his home, and from it. She uses his words, mimics his gestures, acquires his eccentricities and his ties. "I am Heathcliffe," says Catherine in *Wuthering Heights;* that is the cry of every woman in love; she is another incarnation of her loved one, his reflection, his double: she is *he.* She lets her own world collapse in contingence, for she really lives in his.[4]

This may be what Erich Fromm in his *Art of Loving* has called "symbiotic union," but, unlike Fromm's ideal love, it is founded on the cam of the male selfhood.

After he is hurt by the fall of the big gray horse and must be left behind, Jordan tells Maria, "Listen. We will not go to Madrid now but I go always with thee wherever thou goest. Understand?" And again, "Thou wilt go now, rabbit. But I go with thee. As long as there is one of us there is both of us. . . . If thou goest then I go, too. Do you not see how it is? Whichever one there is, is both." She answers,

"I will stay with thee."
"Nay, rabbit. Listen. That people cannot do together. Each one must do it alone. But if thou goest then I go with thee. It is in that way that I go too. Thou wilt go now. I know. For thou art good and kind. Thou wilt go now for us both."

This idea, of course, is as Donneian as the title of Hemingway's book: "Our two souls, therefore, which are one, / Though I must go, endure not yet / A breach, but an expansion, / Like gold to airy thinness beat."[5]

Sartre, too, is fond of it. Milan, in *The Reprieve*, promises his wife Anna that he will not oppose the Free Corps threatening them at the door. She says, "Darling, I know it's for my sake." "No," he says, "not for you. For *you* is really *me*. It's for the child's sake." And Lucie and Jean, in *Morts sans sépulture*, become one for a while. Lucie knows she will die in prison and that Jean, his true identity as a conspirator undiscovered, will be released. "Tomorrow," she says, "you'll go down to the city; you'll take away in your eyes the last look at my face; you'll be the only one in the world to know it. You must not forget it. I am you. If you live, I shall live."

But, says Sartre in *Being and Nothingness*, two can never truly become one, and any attempt to do so is always fraught with the possibility of rupture. The rupture occurs between Lucie and Jean when Lucie is raped by the inquisitors. The act makes her one of those who suffer, and Jean does not suffer. He begs her to "come into my arms and it will become *our* pain." But she is no longer one with him.

Hemingway, too, recognizes the perpetual insecurity of the "I am thee" arrangement. It frightens Catherine when she and Henry drift apart a little way during a slight quarrel. "We really are the same one and we mustn't misunderstand on purpose," she says. "We won't," says Henry. "But people do," she says. "They love each other and they misunderstand on purpose and they fight and then suddenly they aren't the same one."

Immediately following the sleeping-bag episode already mentioned, in which Jordan agrees with Maria that they are one, a Fascist cavalryman rides in upon them suddenly while Rafael, the gypsy who is supposed to be on guard, is killing two hares he found engaged in a love feast. Jordan shoots the cavalryman, pulls up his trousers, and bristles with alertness to any possible subsequent danger. And Hemingway states unequivocally: "She had no place in his life now." Perhaps the death of the two rabbits is symbolic. Regardless, the "I am thee" union is definitely disrupted for Jordan, and even when he tells Maria at the end of the book to go and take him with her one cannot but feel that he is speaking to her as if she were a child believing in a Santa Claus in which he has only pretensions of belief. Though Maria is one of Hemingway's ideal heroines, willing completely to subjugate her life to Jordan's, loving her can never be more than a part of Jordan's life. When the guerrilla band has ridden away, leaving Jordan behind like a humanistic little Christ holding off death for the others, Hemingway says, "They were all gone now and he was alone with his back against a tree." He has told Maria that each must meet death alone; now he sits in Hemingway's typical existential situation—facing death—and thinking little about the girl with whom he has made a love pact.

But lest we typify Hemingway's love stories too simply, attention must be given to another important *affaire d'amour*, that of Brett and Jake in *The Sun Also Rises*. Here we are troubled in our "I am thee" idealism by the fact that the two

persons in the novel who seem inevitably to be lovers are
prevented from that relationship by the physical incapacity of
Jake. Brett is engaged to Mike and becomes wildly enamored
of Romero; yet these are always recognized as passing affairs,
for it is Jake she really loves. Time and again in the novel we
are made aware of a straining togetherward of Brett and Jake,
a mutual yearning always ending in a sense of frustration and
futility.

This piece that is apparently incongruous in the total Hemingway love pattern is not so ill-fitting as it might at first appear.
Actually it supplies further substantiation of Hemingway's view
that it is impossible for both lovers in a mystical union to exist
synchronously as persons. Brett, unlike most Hemingway heroines, is not submerged as a person; with the exception of a
faltering moment when she meets Romero, she remains a
willing, thinking, independent being from first to last. But
had she and Jake been able to consummate their love, it would
have been necessary, according to the code, for one of them
to surrender his personhood, to cease to be a subject and
become an object.[6] This is the rare occasion in a Hemingway
story when a heroine who is admirable by his standards (Brett
would surrender to Jake if Jake could receive the surrender)
remains a person.[7]

It is true that Hemingway's love, even at its most idealistic,
is almost always related to sexual intercourse. That is only
natural for a Nietzschean apostle who believes not in eternity
but in loving the earth; to rob man of God is to make him
revert to a kind of animalism, albeit a special kind, and love
and copulation are difficult to distinguish from one another
on that level. Probably the closest Hemingway's men ever
come to a real acceptance of the two-in-one motif is during the
act of intercourse, when two are actually copulated, at least
physically. For Col. Cantwell, it was "the only mystery he
believed in except the occasional bravery of man."

It may be that Hemingway sees a kind of symbolism in the
sexual act like that of which Beauvoir has spoken; that is, that

the man is on top during intercourse and the being of the
woman is dominated by him. Maria "dies" each time she has
intercourse with Jordan. As St. Paul "died" daily that Christ
might live, she dies to herself and lives in Jordan. But Jordan
says *he* did not die.

Jordan does find, however, that the sexual act is in one
respect curiously like violence and death—it reduces life to
existential simplicity. After two such acts within a period of
eighteen hours or so he can think much more accurately about
politics:

since last night and this afternoon his mind was much clearer and
cleaner on that business. Bigotry is an odd thing. To be bigoted
you have to be absolutely sure you are right and nothing makes
that surety and righteousness like continence. Continence is the foe
of heresy.

And part of the clear thinking of the male after copulation
is his feeling of freedom from the female with whom he has
just participated in the act. It is not so with the female, says
Mme. Beauvoir. When the man moves from her, she finds
herself "back on earth, on a bed, in the light; she again has a
name, a face: she is vanquished, prey, object"; and at the
moment of this lost feeling, love becomes a necessity to her;
she must continue to be part of the man. Maria continues
to be Jordan; but Jordan is never for long Maria.

That is the way love is in a man's world, and Hemingway's
world is such a man's world that it has been called a place
where heroes are known specifically by their genitals.[8] It is
a world where love can never be satisfactory for the Jake
Barneses, because the Brett Ashleys can never be absorbed by
castratos, where true love exists only when a Catherine or a
Maria or a Renata renounces herself in favor of her man, and
where love can never mean everything to the hero because, to
live authentically, he must remain *alone* in the presence of
death.

NOTES

CHAPTER ONE

[1] Young, *Ernest Hemingway* (New York: Rinehart, 1952), p. 2.

[2] Cf. E. M. Halliday, "Hemingway's *In Our Time*," *The Explicator*, VII, No. 5 (March, 1949), Item 35.

[3] *Death in the Afternoon* (New York: Scribner's, 1932), p. 133.

[4] *The Shapers of American Fiction, 1798-1947* (New York: Dutton, 1947), pp. 157-58.

[5] Cf. Wylie Sypher, "*Hamlet*: The Existential Madness," *The Nation*, CLXII (June 22, 1946), 750-51. Hamlet's dismissal of the watch and withdrawal to the lonely tower, his realization that it is in his power to live or to die, his acceptance of the responsibility of removing his father's murderer, his concern for the manner in which it is done, and his disregard for the punishment it might entail, all constitute an existential situation *par excellence*.

[6] These words were written before the author had read Karl Jaspers' sentence in *Reason and Existenz*, "The philosopher of systems is, as a man, like someone who builds a castle, but lives next door in a shanty." Trans. William Earle, in Walter Kaufmann, *Existentialism from Dostoevsky to Sartre* (New York: Meridian, 1956), p. 164.

[7] *Concluding Unscientific Postscript*, trans. David Swenson and Walter Lowrie (Princeton: Princeton University Press, 1941), p. 85.

[8] *Concluding Unscientific Postscript*, p. 296.

[9] Paul Tillich, whose own language is for some readers insurmountable, wrote: " 'Existential' Philosophy seems a specifically German creation. . . . Its terminology has been largely determined by the genius and often by the demon of the German language—a fact which makes the translation of Heidegger's *Sein und Zeit* practically impossible." ("Existential Philosophy," *Journal of the History of Ideas*, V, Jan., 1944, p. 44.)

[10] Cf. Alfred Stern, "Sartre and French Existentialism," *The Personalist*, XXIX, No. 1 (Jan., 1948), 17-31.

[11] *The Thought and Art of Albert Camus* (Chicago: Regnery, 1958), p. 8.

[12] In Colette Audry (ed.), *Pour et Contre l'Existentialisme* (Paris: Atlas, 1948), p. 27.

[13] *Tragic Sense of Life*, trans. J. E. C. Flitch (New York: Dover, 1954), p. 1.

[14] *The Ethics of Ambiguity*, trans. Bernard Frechtman (New York: Philosophical Library, 1948), p. 158.

[15] *Existentialism and Humanism,* trans. E. B. Ashton (New York: Russell F. Moore, 1952), p. 74.

[16] *The Art of Loving* (New York: Harper, 1956), p. 13.

[17] *The Philosophy of Existence,* trans. Manya Harari (New York: Philosophical Library, 1949), p. 2.

[18] *Being and Nothingness,* trans. Hazel Barnes (New York: Philosophical Library, 1956), pp. 30-31. One notes the frequency with which precipices and bridges reappear as leading motifs in existentialist fiction, especially in the work of Sartre. A significant example also appears in Camus' *The Fall,* where Clamence's moments of self-revelation occur on bridges.

[19] John Wild, *The Challenge of Existentialism* (Bloomington: Indiana University Press, 1955), p. 23.

[20] *Being and Nothingness,* pp. 59-60.

[21] J. Glenn Gray, "The Idea of Death in Existentialism," *The Journal of Philosophy;* XLVIII (Mar. 1, 1951), 114.

[22] Cf. Martin Heidegger, "Hölderin and the Essence of Poetry," *Existence and Being,* trans. Werner Brock (London: Vision, 1949).

[23] *The Stranger,* trans. Stuart Gilbert (New York: Knopf, 1948), pp. 130-31.

[24] Cf. Franz Kafka's *The Trial,* from which I believe Camus may have borrowed the idea for *The Stranger.* Joseph K., like Meursault, is bewildered by the conspiracy of the world around him, and eventually kneels above the rock quarry to die "like a dog" at the hands of his plain-man executioners, without ever really learning what crime it is of which he has been guilty.

[25] *Existence and Being,* pp. 365-66.

[26] *Being and Nothingness,* p. 21.

[27] Carlos Baker, *Hemingway; the Writer as Artist* (Princeton: Princeton University Press, 1952), p. 132.

[28] Baker, pp. 124-25.

CHAPTER TWO

[1] "No Beginning and No End: Hemingway and Death," *Essays in Criticism,* III (Jan., 1953), 75.

[2] Granville Hicks, "Twenty Years of Hemingway," *The New Republic,* Oct. 23, 1944, p. 524. Quoted in Thomas H. Cash, Jr., "Ernest Hemingway and Death" (Unpublished M.A. thesis, Dept. of English, University of Kentucky, 1951), p. 4.

[3] *Ernest Hemingway,* pp. 12-13.

[4] Kierkegaard, *Thoughts on Crucial Situations in Human Life,* trans. David Swenson (Minneapolis: Augsburg, 1941), p. 9.

[5] *Thoughts on Crucial Situations,* p. 115.

[6] This is the usual translation of the phrase. Actually, I believe, the translation of *Grenze* as "boundary" is more illuminating.

[7] Cf. E. L. Allen, *The Self and Its Hazards: A Guide to the Thought of Karl Jaspers* (London: Hodder and Stoughton, 1953), pp. 32-33, for a brief discussion of these particular limit-situations.

8 *The Reprieve,* trans. Eric Sutton (New York: Knopf, 1947), pp. 364-65.

9 *The Myth of Sisyphus,* trans. Justin O'Brien (London: Hamish Hamilton, 1955), p. 11.

10 "In Another Country," *The Fifth Column and the First Forty-Nine Stories* (New York: Scribner's, 1938).

11 *Ernest Hemingway,* pp. 12-13. Cf. Edmund Wilson, "Ernest Hemingway: Bourdon Gauge of Morale," *The Atlantic Monthly,* CLXIV (July, 1939), 36. Wilson also sees that there is really a connection between the apparently disparate experiences of the boy Nick and the soldier with the spine wound, that there is a current of violence coursing through his whole life, through the Indian camp, the war, and even the angling on Big Two-Hearted River: "The condition of life is pain; and the joys of the most innocent surface are somehow tied to its stifled pangs."

12 *Concluding Unscientific Postscript,* p. 79.

13 *Fear and Trembling,* trans. Robert Payne (London: Oxford University Press, 1939), p. 34.

14 *The Myth of Sisyphus,* p. 47.

15 *Being and Nothingness,* pp. 37, 441.

16 Freud borrowed the term "nirvana-principle" from Barbara Low to apply to the death impulse, nirvana being a Sanskrit word meaning "to blow out," *i.e.,* to extinguish the sensations. Later, the life and death instincts were known as Eros and Thanatos, respectively, although Freud used the latter term only in conversation and not in writing.

17 *Beyond the Pleasure Principle,* trans. C. J. M. Hubback (London: International Psycho-Analytical Press, 1922), pp. 43-44. As Ernest Jones points out in his monumental *Life and Work of Sigmund Freud* (New York: Basic Books, 1957), the theory of the death instinct has been discounted by most modern psychologists, with a few notable exceptions, among them Karl Menninger of the famous Menninger Foundation. Dr. Menninger's eminently readable volume *Man Against Himself* is a 400-page variation on the single theme, "Each man has his own way of destroying himself; some are more expedient than others, some more consciously deliberate than others."

18 *Death in the Afternoon,* p. 2.

19 *The Rebel,* trans. Anthony Bower (New York: Knopf, 1954), p. 251.

20 Compare also the occasion in "The Snows of Kilimanjaro" where Harry bickers with Helen and makes her cry. "Listen," he says. "Do you think that it is fun to do this? I don't know why I'm doing it. It's trying to kill to keep yourself alive, I imagine."

21 *Death in the Afternoon,* pp. 232-33.

22 *Green Hills of Africa* (New York: Scribner's, 1953), p. 120.

23 *Death in the Afternoon,* p. 68.

CHAPTER THREE

1 *Existentialism,* trans. Bernard Frechtman (New York: Philosophical Library, 1947), p. 27.

[2] Cf. *Being and Nothingness*, pp. 50, 65.

[3] *The Ethics of Ambiguity*, p. 47. The word *facticity* was evidently coined by Beauvoir's translator to mean objectivity or factness; it now has some currency among those writing in English on the subject of existentialism.

[4] *The Second Sex*, trans. H. M. Parshley (New York: Knopf, 1953), p. 385.

[5] *The Reprieve*, p. 133. The French title of this book (*Le Sursis*) is significant: the final characters of all the persons in the book are held in suspense while they make the choices determining what they shall be.

[6] *The Reprieve*, p. 407.

[7] *The Sickness unto Death*, trans. Walter Lowrie (Princeton: Princeton University Press, 1941), p. 51.

[8] Cf. Maxwell Geismar, "No Man Alone Now," *The Virginia Quarterly Review*, XVII, No. 4 (Oct., 1941), 518.

[9] *Death in the Afternoon*, pp. 7-8.

[10] As reported by Hemingway, the words are, "No, no, let us cross over the river and rest under the shade of the trees."

[11] *The Virginia Quarterly Review*, XIII (Jan., 1937), 116.

[12] *Dostoevsky*, trans. Donald Attwater (New York: Meridian, 1957), p. 114.

[13] "Ernest Hemingway: Bourdon Gauge of Morale," *The Atlantic Monthly*, CLXIV (July, 1939), 45.

[14] Cf. Joseph Whitt, "Hemingway's 'The End of Something,'" *The Explicator*, IX (June, 1951), No. 8, Item 58. Whitt's interpretation of Nick's separation from Marjorie is that Nick has "unexpressed homosexual tendencies" and therefore chooses Bill over Marjorie. Granted the correctness of the Freudian hypotheses back of Whitt's statement, I would be inclined to agree with him. However, this does not alter the importance of Nick's decision relative to the thesis of this chapter.

[15] This is also the theme of Kierkegaard's "The Lilies of the Field," in *The Gospel of Suffering and the Lilies of the Field*, trans. David and Lillian Swenson (Minneapolis: Augsburg, 1948).

[16] Benoit Pruche, *L'Homme de Sartre* (Paris: Arthaud, 1949), p. 21, says of Orestes' exit: "Libre, Oreste est à jamais seul et l'angoisse est son lot."

[17] Cf. Baker, *Hemingway*, p. 95; Malcolm Cowley, "Hemingway and the Hero," *The New Republic*, CXI (Dec. 4, 1944), 756.

[18] *Reason and Existenz*, in Kaufmann, *Existentialism*, pp. 165, 168.

[19] Cf. Charles A. Fenton, *The Apprenticeship of Ernest Hemingway* (New York: Farrar, Straus and Young, 1954), for the history of Hemingway's employment as a journalist.

[20] In one of Hemingway's most recent stories, "Get a Seeing-Eyed Dog" (*The Atlantic Monthly*, Nov., 1957), a husband and wife have barred certain words and phrases from their speech as meaningless. The husband uses the word palpable, then says, "That's a new word and we'll bar it soon."

[21] *What is Literature?* trans. Bernard Frechtman (New York: Philosophical Library, 1949), pp. 210-11.

[22] *Sartre: Romantic Rationalist* (New Haven: Yale University Press, 1953), p. 26.

23 *Fear and Trembling*, p. 63.
24 Camus, *The Myth of Sisyphus*, p. 47.

CHAPTER FOUR

1 *Thus Spake Zarathustra*, trans. A. Tille (New York: Dutton, 1933), p. 69.
2 Cf. Camus, *The Rebel*, p. 60; E. L. Allen, *Existentialism from Within* (New York: Macmillan, 1953), p. 49; James D. Collins, *The Existentialists, A Critical Study* (Chicago: Regnery, 1952), pp. 168-69.
3 Collins, *The Existentialists*, p. 64.
4 *The Myth of Sisyphus*, p. 45.
5 I am following the interpretive suggestion of Walter Kaufmann, *Existentialism*, p. 122.
6 *The Fifth Column*.
7 Cf. *A Farewell to Arms*, Chapter II.
8 Cf. *Green Hills of Africa*, p. 38.
9 Dostoievski, *The Brothers Karamazov*.
10 *Encounter with Nothingness* (Hinsdale, Illinois: Regnery, 1949), p. xvii.
11 *The Myth of Sisyphus*, pp. 49-50, 52.
12 *The Will to Power*, trans. A. M. Ludovici (New York: Macmillan, 1924), p. 127.
13 "The Missing All," *The Virginia Quarterly Review*, XIII (Jan., 1937), 118.
14 Maurice Natanson, "Jean-Paul Sartre's Philosophy of Freedom," *Social Research*, XIX (Sept., 1952), 378.
15 Allen, *The Self and Its Hazards*, p. 7.
16 *Thus Spake Zarathustra*, p. 24.
17 *Being and Nothingness*, pp. 92-4.
18 *L'Existentialisme et la sagesse des nations* (Paris: Nagel, 1948), pp. 92-3.
19 *Man for Himself* (New York: Rinehart, 1947), pp. 20, 44-5. Fromm read Sartre's *Flies* and *Is Existentialism a Humanism?* while he was revising the manuscript of this book, and probably derived his title from Sartre's *pour-soi* category. Although he is not an existentialist himself, he is in basic agreement with the ethical position of existentialism.
20 *Concluding Unscientific Postscript*, pp. 127, 284, 291.
21 *Tragic Sense of Life*, pp. 261, 263.
22 Cf. *Being and Nothingness*, p. 39.
23 Sartre, *Existentialism*, p. 19. Sartre calls this the doctrine of "forlornness," and assigns it as the reason that existentialism proves too demanding for most people.
24 Cf. Fadiman's "Ernest Hemingway: An American Byron," *The Nation*, CXXXV (1933), 63-64.
25 "Novelist-Philosophers," *Horizon*, XV (April, 1947), 163.
26 Alfred Stern, "Sartre and French Existentialism," pp. 30-31.
27 Oliver Evans, "The Rise of Existentialism," *The South Atlantic Quarterly*, XLVII, No. 2 (April, 1948), 156.
28 *Death in the Afternoon*, p. 91.

[29] *Concluding Unscientific Postscript*, p. 314.

[30] "Ernest Hemingway and Death," p. 35.

[31] "He who dies on Thursday does not have to die on Friday."

[32] Cf. Pablo's disappointment in the priest who died "very badly," *For Whom the Bell Tolls*, chapter X; *The Fifth Column*, II, i.

[33] *The Rebel*, p. 21. Hemingway had used the phrase earlier, in *For Whom the Bell Tolls*, putting it in the mouth of Joaquin, one of the guerrillas who die with Sordo. Joaquin attributes it to Pasionaria, a female propagandist for the Communists.

[34] Paul-Louis Landsberg, *The Experience of Death and The Moral Problem of Suicide*, trans. Cynthia Rowland (New York: Philosophical Library, 1953), p. 49.

[35] *Green Hills of Africa*, pp. 37-38.

[36] *The Myth of Sisyphus*, p. 11.

[37] *Ernest Hemingway*, p. 40.

[38] "On the Blue Water" was published in *Esquire*, V (Apr., 1936), 31, 184-85. Cf. Young, *Ernest Hemingway*, p. 95.

CHAPTER FIVE

[1] *The Virginia Quarterly Review*, XVII, No. 4 (Oct., 1941), 517-34.

[2] *L'Homme de Sartre*, p. 53. "Oreste, lui, *assume* son acte, sa conduit criminelle, et cet acte l'engage. Assumant son acte, il ne cesse de reprendre son choix libre, et 'c'est le point du jour': son crime est le début de *sa* liberté, de *son* existence. Assumant son acte, celui-ci-ne pese pas, si lourd soit-il, car il est vraimant *son acte*, le sien: 'J'ai fait *mon* acte.'"

[3] *Existentialism*, pp. 19-20.

[4] *The Ethics of Ambiguity*, p. 71.

[5] *Reason and Existenz*, in Kaufmann, *Existentialism*, p. 147.

[6] Ralph Harper, *Existentialism: A Theory of Man* (Cambridge: Harvard University Press, 1948), pp. 102-103.

[7] *The Concept of Dread*, trans. Walter Lowrie (Princeton: Princeton University Press, 1946), p. 26, fn.

[8] *Tragic Sense of Life*, p. 24.

[9] *Existentialism and Humanism*, pp. 20-21.

[10] Beauvoir, *The Ethics of Ambiguity*, pp. 99, 110.

[11] "La République du Silence," *Situations III* (Paris: Gallimard, 1949), pp. 11-14.

[12] *The Ethics of Ambiguity*, p. 107.

[13] *Being and Nothingness*, p. 554.

CHAPTER SIX

[1] *Being and Nothingness*, p. 364. Cf. also Marjorie Grene, *Dreadful Freedom; A Critique of Existentialism* (Chicago: University of Chicago Press, 1948), p. 83.

2 *L'Homme de Sartre*, p. 118.

3 *The Second Sex*, p. 642.

4 *The Second Sex*, p. 653. It should be noted that for Beauvoir this statement is descriptive, but for Hemingway it is normative.

5 John Donne, "A Valediction Forbidding Mourning."

6 Unable to have sexual relations with her real love, Brett does have them with others, but except for Romero they are objects, not subjects. Romero is different. She first fights down his attempt to destroy her—he wants her to let her hair grow, dress like other women, and marry him—and then she must leave him before she destroys *him*. It is this decision to leave that makes her feel good—the decision not to be "one of those bitches that ruins children."

7 Marjorie, Mrs. Macomber and Dorothy are "bad" for the Hemingway men because they actually become their rivals in the attempt to exist as individuals.

8 Cf. Lincoln Kirstein, "The Canon of Death," in *Ernest Hemingway: The Man and His Work*, p. 60.

CONCLUSION

1 Baker, *Hemingway*, p. 193.

2 William Phillips, "Male-ism and Moralism," *The American Mercury*, LXXV (Oct., 1952), 97-98.

3 James T. Farrell, "The Sun Also Rises," in *Ernest Hemingway: The Man and His Work*, p. 225.

4 *Reason and Existenz*, in Kaufmann, *Existentialism*, p. 197.

INDEX

Abelard, Peter, 99, 100
Abel Sanchez, 35
Absurd, the, 26, 50
Across the River and into the Trees, 38, 39, 81, 98. *See also* Cantwell, Richard; Renata
Adams, Nick, 2, 17, 18, 19, 22-24, 28, 31, 43, 47, 51, 58, 59, 60, 70, 71, 81, 98, 106n
Age of Reason, The, 20
Ahab, 25, 63
"Alpine Idyll, An," 70
Ambassadors, The, 66
Angst, 14, 26. *See also* Anguish
Anguish, 14, 30, 106n. *See also Angst*
Anselmo, 58-59, 86
Ashley, Brett, 60, 66, 94, 95, 96, 100, 109n

Bad faith, 11, 34, 37
"Banal Story," 71
Barnes, Jake, 15, 23, 24, 31, 39-40, 58, 66, 68, 94, 95, 96, 99, 100
"Battler, The," 22, 27, 51
Beauvoir, Simone de, 5, 6, 7, 34, 61, 64, 65, 84, 85, 87, 90, 92, 95-99 *passim*, 101. *See also Mandarins, The*
Being and Nothingness, 4, 8, 14, 19, 57, 93
Being-for-itself, 11, 51, 54, 107n
Being-in-itself, 11, 51, 54
Berdyaev, Nicholas, 5
Bierce, Ambrose, 54
"Big Two-Hearted River," 58, 71
Brothers Karamazov, The, 56. *See also* Karamazov, Ivan; Zossima, Father
Buber, Martin, 5

Bullfights, 22, 28-29, 30, 31, 37, 39, 51, 58, 63, 67-68, 78, 98
Bultmann, Rudolph, 5

Camus, Albert, 4-5, 16, 21, 22, 26, 29, 50, 57, 61, 67, 76, 77, 83, 97, 98, 99, 101. *See also Fall, The; Meursault; Plague, The; Stranger, The*
"Canary for One," 38, 40
Cantwell, Richard, 1, 15, 23, 24, 39-41, 62, 68, 69, 72, 75, 76, 81, 83, 84, 91, 95, 98
Castle, The, 57
Chemins de la liberté, Les, 35, 82
Choice, 6, 10-11, 12, 16, 97-98
Christ, 55, 56, 58, 79, 80. *See also* Jesus
Christological imagery, 80
"Clean, Well-Lighted Place, A," 14, 58
Cohn, Robert, 39-40, 68
Crane, Stephen, 48
Critique of Pure Reason, 5
"Cross-Country Snow," 47, 70

Darkness: as symbol, 58
Dasein, 10-11, 20
"Day's Wait, A," 25
Death: equated with violence, 17; Hemingway's preoccupation with, 17-18; key to Hemingway's philosophy, 18; and sin, 19; as revealer of freedom, 19; anticipation of, 20; of Mathieu Delarue, 20; as seen by Hemingway's heroes, 22-24; in the bullring, 28, 76; of Richard Cantwell, 41; of Catherine Henry, 46-48; and nausea, 51-54; the smell

Death (*continued*):
of, 52-54; and form, 69-70; of the lion, 76; of the hyena, 76-77; mentioned, 36, 37, 63, 75. *See also Sein zum Tode;* Suicide
Death instinct, 27, 105n
Death in the Afternoon, 37, 48, 49, 58, 66, 78
De Beauvoir, Simone. *See* Beauvoir, Simone de
Delarue, Mathieu, 19-20, 22, 36, 47, 67, 82, 83
De Unamuno, Miguel. *See* Unamuno, Miguel de
"Doctor and the Doctor's Wife, The," 22
Donne, John, 17, 85, 93
Dostoievski, Fyodor, 3, 43, 56
Dread. *See Angst;* Anguish

Eliot, T. S., 38, 48, 49, 63
"End of Something, The," 43
Ethics, 16, 61, 64-67, 69, 80, 98, 101
Ethics of Ambiguity, The, 87
Être et avoir, 44

Fadiman, Clifton, 66
Fall, The, 82-83, 104n
Farewell to Arms, A, 27, 46, 47-48, 49, 60, 83, 89. *See also* Henry, Catherine; Henry, Frederick
Farrell, James T., 100
"Fathers and Sons," 23, 51
Fifth Column, The, 81, 85. *See also* Rawlings, Philip
Ford, Ford Madox, 89
Form: and *pundonor*, 69; in skiing, 70; in fishing, 71, 73-74; in lovemaking, 72; in selecting food, 72-73; in living, 73; in hunting, 74-75; in dying, 75-79
For Whom the Bell Tolls, 27, 48, 52, 71, 77, 81, 84, 85, 89, 91. *See also* Anselmo; Jordan, Robert; Maria; Pilar
Freedom: to be or not to be, 11; appears in moment of anguish, 19, 106n; revealed by death, 19, 35; as freedom to kill, 29; as man's nature,

Freedom (*continued*):
34; from moral traditions, 61; requires freedom of all, 84-86, 99; mentioned, 26, 32, 43, 82
Freud, Sigmund, 27, 105n
Fromm, Erich: on the passing of individualism, 8-9; and humanistic ethics, 64-65; and symbiotic union, 92; and Sartre, 107n

"Gambler, the Nun, and the Radio, The," 37, 78
"Get a Seeing-Eyed Dog," 106n
"God Rest Ye Merry, Gentlemen," 84
Green Hills of Africa, 37-38, 42, 63, 68, 74

Hamlet, 2, 103n
Hartmann, Nicolai, 64
Hawthorne, Nathaniel, 64
Hegel, G. W. F., 2, 3, 7, 8, 25, 57, 100
Heidegger, Martin, 3-4, 5, 10, 11, 12, 15, 16, 34, 54, 55, 97, 98. *See also Sein und Zeit; Sein zum Tode*
Hemingway, Ernest: identification with his characters, 31, 41, 47, 68, 77, 91, 98
Henry, Catherine, 28, 46-48, 90, 91, 94, 96
Henry, Frederick, 2, 23, 24, 28, 31, 46-48, 58, 60, 63, 78, 81, 83, 89, 94, 99
"Hills Like White Elephants," 47, 83
Hölderin, 12
Huis Clos. See No Exit

Ilyich, Iván, 21
"In Another Country," 29
"Indian Camp," 17, 52, 70, 77
Individualism, 6-10, 12, 24-27, 41, 42, 64, 88, 97
In Our Time, 1, 18, 23, 51
Iron in the Soul, 20

Jackson (Cantwell's orderly), 39-41
James, Henry, 66, 97

Jaspers, Karl, 5, 6, 8, 19, 22, 36, 48, 54, 84, 85, 97, 101
Jesus, 2. *See also* Christ
Jordan, Robert, 1, 23, 24, 26, 28, 31, 52-54, 68, 77, 84, 86, 87, 88, 91, 94, 96, 99
Jung, C. G., 58

Kafka, Franz, 57, 67. *See also* "Metamorphosis"
Kant, Emmanuel. *See Critique of Pure Reason*
Karamazov, Ivan, 56, 62, 67
Kierkegaard, Søren, 2-3, 5, 6, 7, 10, 16, 19, 25, 34, 36, 38, 50, 57, 65, 67, 69, 85, 97
"Killers, The," 22
Killing, 29-30, 105n
Krebs, 24, 33-34, 41, 51, 98

Language: too complicated, 48-49, 106n
Leap of faith, 5, 57
Leavittown, 8
L'Être et le néant. See Being and Nothingness
Lewis, Sinclair, 38
Limit-situations, 19, 22, 54
Love: of Nick and Marjorie, 43; of Catherine and Henry, 91, 94; of Cantwell and Renata, 91; of Jordan and Maria, 91-92, 93, 94, 96, 99; of Brett and Jake, 94-95; mentioned, 62, 63, 89, 90, 99

Macomber, Francis, 44-46, 75
Macomber, Margot, 45, 90, 109n
Maera (Manuel Garcia), 78
Mains sales, Les, 86
Malingering, 83
Mandarins, The, 88
Marcel, Gabriel, 5, 8, 9-10, 36, 97. *See also Être et avoir*
Maria, 68, 90, 91, 94, 96, 99
Maritain, Jacques, 5
Marjorie, 43, 90, 106n, 109n
Mass man, vii, 8, 25, 36
Men at War, 75

Mencken, H. L., 40
Men Without Women, 43, 89
"Metamorphosis," 12
Meursault, 12-13, 67, 104n
Moby-Dick, 24-25. *See also* Ahab
Moment of truth, 30, 31, 32, 33, 51, 54, 58
Morgan, Harry, 24, 27, 44, 52, 68, 73, 77, 81, 84
Morts sans sépulture, 26, 67, 93
Mouches, Les, 20, 48. *See also* Orestes
"Mr. and Mrs. Elliot," 38
Myth of Sisyphus, The, 50, 61

Nada, vii, 14-15, 32, 58
"Natural History of the Dead, A," 1, 22
Nausea, 34, 50-54
Nausée, La, 50-51
Nietzsche, Friedrich, 3, 6, 7, 13, 55, 56, 57, 61, 62, 63, 64, 98. *See also* Superman; Zarathustra
No Exit, 9, 20, 57, 65
Nothingness, 14-15, 19. *See also Nada*
"Now I Lay Me," 71

Old Man and the Sea, The, 17, 23, 24, 52, 80, 81, 88. *See also* Santiago
"On the Quai at Smyrna," 22
Orestes, 20, 48, 57, 82, 108n
Organization Man, The, 8
Ortega y Gasset, 5

Paris, France, vii, 5, 31
Pilar, 52-54, 71-72
Plague, The, 21, 82. *See also* Rambert
Poe, Edgar Allan, 54
Pundonor, 67-68, 69, 79, 99
"Pursuit Race, A," 51

Rain: as symbol, 48
Rambert, 21
Rawlings, Philip, 15, 58, 85, 87
Rebel, 12, 26. *See also* Revolt
Religion, 33, 35, 37, 55, 58, 60, 61, 75, 99

Renata, 38, 69, 90, 91, 96
Repetition-compulsion, 27
Reprieve, The, 19, 20, 57, 67, 93, 106n
"Republic of Silence, The," 87
Revolt, 5, 76. *See also* Rebel
Romero, 29, 60, 109n

Samsa, Gregor. *See* "Metamorphosis"
Santiago, 17, 24, 26, 48, 52, 60, 63, 79, 80, 98, 99
Sartre, Jean-Paul, vii, 4, 5, 8, 9, 10, 11, 14, 15, 16, 19-20, 26, 34, 36, 49, 50, 54, 57, 64, 65, 67, 83, 84, 87, 88, 90, 93, 97, 98, 99, 101. *See also* Being-for-itself; *Chemins de la liberté, Les;* Delarue, Mathieu; *Mains sales, Les; Mouches, Les; Nausée, La*
Second Sex, The, 34-35
Sein und Zeit, 3-4, 20, 103n
Sein zum Tode, 20, 22, 54, 98
Separate peace, 2, 14, 18, 24, 81, 88, 89
"Short Happy Life of Francis Macomber, The," 44-46, 75, 76. *See also* Macomber, Margot
Sickness unto death, 36
"Snows of Kilimanjaro, The," 43, 60, 71, 99, 105n
Socrates, 2, 3, 69
"Soldier's Home," 33-34, 51. *See also* Krebs
Stein, Gertrude, 48, 62
Stoicism, 2
Stranger, The, 82, 104n. *See also* Meursault
Sub-men, 34
Suicide, 5, 21, 23, 77, 83

Sun Also Rises, The, 28, 29, 37, 59-60, 66, 94
Superman, 3, 55, 57

Thélèmites, 65
"Three-Day Blow, The," 43
Thoreau, Henry David, 2
Tillich, Paul, 5, 103n
"Today is Friday," 79
To Have and Have Not, 44, 47, 52, 73, 85. *See also* Morgan, Harry
Tragic Sense of Life, 8, 14
Trial, The, 104n
Twain, Mark, 48

Unamuno, Miguel de, 5, 6, 15, 65, 85, 97. *See also Abel Sanchez; Tragic Sense of Life*

"Very Short Story, A," 51
Violence: equated with death, 17, 18; in life of Nick Adams, 22-24, 105n; and nausea, 51. *See also* Death; Wound
Vorhandenheit, 10-11

Waste Land, The, 38
Whyte, William H., 8
Womb symbols, 27, 48
Wound, 23-24, 39, 41, 76, 98, 105n. *See also* Death; Violence

Zarathustra, 55, 57, 62
Zola, Émile, 54
Zossima, Father, 62

JOHN KILLINGER, the author of this book, is a graduate of Baylor University and holds the S.T.B. degree from Harvard University and the Ph.D. degree from the University of Kentucky. He is now assistant professor of English at Georgetown College, Kentucky.

HEMINGWAY AND THE DEAD GODS was composed and printed at the University of Kentucky. It is set in Linotype Caledonia, with headings in Klingspor Kumlein. The book is printed on Warren's Olde Style antique wove paper and bound by the C. J. Krehbiel Company in Columbia's Bayside Vellum cloth.